# ADRIFT IN THE WILDS

OR, The Adventures of Two Shipwrecked Boys

## EDWARD S. ELLIS

1st WORLD
LIBRARY
Literary Society

# Adrift in the Wilds

Edward S. Ellis

© 1st World Library, 2007
PO Box 2211
Fairfield, IA 52556
www.1stworldlibrary.com
First Edition

LCCN: 2007930743

Softcover ISBN: 978-1-4218-4813-6
Hardcover ISBN: 978-1-4218-4716-0
eBook ISBN: 978-1-4218-4910-2

Purchase *"Adrift in the Wilds"*
as a traditional bound book at:
www.1stWorldLibrary.com/purchase.asp?ISBN=978-1-4218-4813-6

1st World Library is a literary, educational organization
dedicated to:

- Creating a free internet library of downloadable ebooks

- Hosting writing competitions and offering book publishing
scholarships.

Interested in more 1st World Library books? contact:
literacy@1stworldlibrary.com
Check us out at: www.1stworldlibrary.com

# 1ˢᵗ World Library Literary Society

## Giving Back to the World

"If you want to work on the core problem, it's early school literacy."

**- James Barksdale, former CEO of Netscape**

"No skill is more crucial to the future of a child, or to a democratic and prosperous society, than literacy."

**- Los Angeles Times**

"Literacy... means far more than learning how to read and write... The aim is to transmit... knowledge and promote social participation."

**- UNESCO**

"Literacy is not a luxury, it is a right and a responsibility. If our world is to meet the challenges of the twenty-first century we must harness the energy and creativity of all our citizens."

**- President Bill Clinton**

"Parents should be encouraged to read to their children, and teachers should be equipped with all available techniques for teaching literacy, so the varying needs and capacities of individual kids can be taken into account."

**- Hugh Mackay**

# CHAPTER I

## HO, FOR CALIFORNIA

One beautiful misummer night in 18—a large, heavily laden steamer was making her way swiftly up the Pacific coast, in the direction of San Francisco. She was opposite the California shore, only a day's sail distant from the City of the Golden Gate, and many of the passengers had already begun making preparations for landing, even though a whole night and the better part of a day was to intervene ere they could expect to set their feet upon solid land.

She was one of those magnificent steamers that ply regularly between Panama and California. She had rather more than her full cargo of freight and passengers; but, among the hundreds of the latter, we have to do with but three.

On this moonlight night, there were gathered by themselves these three personages, consisting of Tim O'Rooney, Elwood Brandon and Howard Lawrence. The first was a burly, good-natured Irishman, and the two latter were cousins, their ages differing by less than a month, and both being in their sixteenth year.

The financial storm that swept over the country in 18—, toppling down merchants and banking-houses like so many ten-pins, carried with it in the general wreck and ruin, that of Brandon, Herman & Co., and the senior partner, Sylvanus Brandon, returned to his home in Brooklyn, New York, one evening worse than penniless. While he was meditating, dejected and gloomy, as to the means by which he was to keep the wolf from the door, his clerk brought him a letter which had been overlooked in the afternoon's mail, postmarked, "San Francisco, Cal." At once he recognized the bold, handsome superscription as that of his kind-hearted brother-in-law, Thomas Lawrence. His heart beat with a strong hope as he broke the envelope, and his eyes glistened ere he had read one-half.

In short, it stated that Mr. Lawrence had established himself successfully in business, and was doing so well that he felt the imperative need of a partner, and ended by urging Mr. Brandon to accept the position. The bankrupt merchant laid the epistle in his lap, removed his spectacles and looked smilingly toward his wife. They held a long discussion, and both decided to accept the offer at once, as there was no other recourse left to them.

It was evident from the letter that Mr. Lawrence had some apprehensions regarding Mr. Brandon's ability to weather the storm, but he could not be aware of his financial crash, as it had only become known on the street within the last twenty-four hours. Mr. Brandon deemed it proper, therefore, before closing with the offer, to acquaint his brother-in-law with his circumstances, that he might fully understand the disadvantage under which he would be placed by the new partnership.

The letter was written and duly posted, and our friends rather anxiously awaited the answer. It came in the gratifying form of a draft for $1,000 to defray "his necessary expenses," and an urgent entreaty to start without delay.

The advice was acted upon, and within two weeks of the reception of the second letter, Mr. Brandon and his wife were on board the steamer at New York, with their state-rooms engaged for California. They had but one child, Elwood, whom they had placed at a private school where he was to prepare himself for college, in company with his cousin, Howard Lawrence, who had been sent from California by his father and had entered the school at the same time.

Mr. Brandon learned that Mr. Lawrence was a brother indeed. The position in which the two men were placed proved so favorable to the former that in a few years he found himself almost as wealthy as in his palmiest days, when his name was such a power in Wall Street. He had come to like the young and growing State of California, and ere he had been there two years both himself and wife had lost all longings for the metropolis of the New World.

In the meanwhile, Elwood and Howard were doing well at their studies in Brooklyn. They had been inseparable friends from infancy, and as their years increased the bonds of affection seemed to strengthen between them. They were the only children of twin sisters, and bore a remarkable resemblance in person, character and disposition. Both had dark, curling, chestnut hair, hazel eyes, and an active muscular organization that made them leaders in boyish pastimes and sports. If there was any perceptible difference between the two, it was that Elwood Brandon was a little more daring and impetuous than his companion; he was apt to follow out his first impulses and venture upon schemes without deliberating fully enough. Both were generous, unselfish, and either would have willingly risked his life for the other.

Thus matters stood until the summer when our young heroes

had completed their preparatory course, and were ready to enter college. It was decided by their parents that this should be done in the autumn, and that the summer of this year should be spent by the boys with their parents in California. They had been separated from them for five years, during which they had met but once, when the parents made a journey to New York for that purpose, spending several months with them. That visit, it may be said, was now to be returned, and the boys meant that it should be returned with interest.

And so Tim O'Rooney, a good-natured, trustworthy Irishman, who had been in the employ of Mr. Lawrence for eight years, almost ever since his arrival in America, was sent to New York to accompany the boys on their visit home.

Howard and Elwood were standing one afternoon on the corner of Montague Street, in Brooklyn, chatting with each other about their expected trip to California. They had closed their school studies a week before, and boy-like were now anxious to be off upon their journey. Suddenly an Irishman came in sight, smoking furiously at a short black pipe. The first glance showed them that it was no other than Tim O'Rooney, the expected messenger.

"Isn't that good?" exclaimed Elwood, "the steamer sails on Saturday, and we'll go in it. Here he comes, as though he was in a great hurry!"

"Don't say anything, and see whether he will know us!"

"Why shouldn't he?"

"You know we've grown a good deal since he was here, and the beard is getting so stiff on my chin that it scratches my hand every time I touch it."

Edward S. Ellis

"Yes; that mustache, too, is making you look as fierce as a Bluebeard; but here he is!"

At this instant Tim O'Rooney came opposite them. He merely glanced up, puffed harder than ever and was passing on, when both burst out in a loud laugh.

"Be the powers! what's the mather with ye spalpeens?" he angrily demanded. "Can't a dacent man be passing the sthrats widout being insulted—Howly mother! is it yerselves or is it your grandfathers?"

He had recognized them, and a hearty hand-shaking followed. Tim grinned a great deal over his mistake, and answered their questions in his dry, witty way, and assured them that his instructions were to bring them home as soon as possible. Accordingly, they embarked on the steamer on the following Saturday; and, passing over the unimportant incidents of their voyage, we come back to our starting point, where all three were within a day's journey of their destination.

# CHAPTER II

## FIRE

"To-morrow we shall be home," said Elwood Brandon, addressing his companion, although at the time he was looking out on the moon-lit sea, in the direction of California.

"Yes; if nothing unexpected happens," replied his cousin, who was pushing and drawing a large Newfoundland dog that lay at his feet.

"And what can happen?" asked his cousin, turning abruptly toward him.

"A hundred things. Suppose the boiler should blow up, we run on a rock, take fire, or get struck by a squall—"

"Or be carried away in a balloon," was the impatient exclamation. "One is just as likely to happen as the other."

"Hardly—heigh-ho!"

Howard at that moment had twined his feet around the neck of Terror, the Newfoundland, and the mischievous dog, springing suddenly to his feet, brought his master from his seat to the deck, which, as a matter of course, made both of the cousins laugh.

"He did that on purpose," said Howard, recovering his position.

"Of course he did. You have been pestering him for the last half-hour, and he is getting tired of it; but I may say, Howard, I shall hardly be able to sleep to-night, I am so anxious to see father and mother."

"So am I; a few years makes such a difference in us, while I can't detect the least change in them."

"Except a few more gray hairs, or perhaps an additional wrinkle or two. What's the matter with Tim?"

"Tim! O nothing, he seems to be meditating and smoking. Fact is that is about all he has done since he has been with us."

"It's been a grand time for Tim, and I have no doubt he has enjoyed the trip to and from California as much as either of us."

The subject of these remarks was seated a few feet away, his arms folded, while he was looking with a vague, dreamy expression out upon the great Pacific, stretching so many thousand miles beyond them, rolling far off in each direction, until sky and ocean blended in great gloom.

"Maybe he is looking for Asia," laughed Elwood in an undertone.

"More likely he is hoping to get a glimpse of Ireland, for he would be as likely to look in that direction as any other. I say, Tim!"

The Irishman did not heed the call until he was addressed the second time in a louder tone than before, when he suddenly raised his head.

"Whisht! what is it?"

"What are you thinking about?"

"Nothin', I was dreaming."

"Dreaming! what about?"

"Begorrah but that was a qua'r dream, was that same one."

"Let's hear it."

"But it's onplaiasnt."

"Never mind, out with it."

"Well, thin, if I must tell yees, I was thinking that this owld staamer was all on fire, and all of us passengers was jumping around in the wather, pulling each other down, away miles into the sea, till we was gone so long there wasn't a chance iver to git up agin."

A strange fear thrilled both of the boys at the mention of this, and they looked at each other a moment in silence.

"What put that into your head, Tim?"

"And it's just the question I was axing meself, for I never draamed of such a thing in my life before, and it's mighty qua'r that I should take a notion to do it now."

"It ain't worth talking about," said Elwood, showing an

anxiety to change the subject.

"Be yees going to bed to-night?"

"I don't feel a bit sleepy," replied Elwood. "I'd just as soon sit up half the night as not."

"And so would I; it must be after eleven o'clock, isn't it?"

"It's near 'levin," replied Tim. "I'm not able to examine me watch; and if I was, I couldn't tell very well, as it hasn't run for a few months."

Howard took out his watch, but the moonlight was too faint for him to distinguish the hands, and the three were content to let the precise time remain a matter of conjecture.

"Tim, how close are we to land?" asked Elwood.

"I should say about the same distance that the land is from us, and begorrah that's the best information I can give yees."

"I could see the mountains very plainly when the sun was setting," said Howard, "and it cannot be many miles away."

"What sort of a country is it off here?" pursued Elwood, pointing in the direction of the land.

"It is wild and rocky, and there are plenty of Indians and wild animals there."

"How do you know?" asked Elwood, in some amazement.

"I have taken the trouble to learn all about California that I could before coming."

"I believe they have *gold* there?" said Elwood, in rather a bantering vein.

"Tim can tell you more about that than I can, as he came to California to hunt gold."

"How is that, Tim?"

"Begorrah, but he shpakes the truth. I wint up among the mountains to hunt gowld."

"And what luck had you?"

"Luck, is it?" repeated the Irishman, with an expression of ludicrous disgust. "Luck, does ye call it, to have your head cracked and your shins smashed by the copper-skins, chawed up by the b'ars, froze to death in the mountains, drowned in the rivers—that run into the top of yer shanty when yer sound asleep—your feet gnawed off by wolverines, as they call—and—but whisht! don't talk to me of luck, and all the time ye never gets a sight of a particle of gowld."

The boys laughed, Howard said:

"But your luck is not every one's, Tim; there have been plenty who have made fortunes at the business."

"Yis, but they wasn't Tim O'Rooneys. He's not the man that was born to be rich!"

"You're better satisfied where you are."

"Yis, thank God, that I've such a good home, and an ongrateful dog would I baa if I should ask more."

"But, Elwood, it's getting late, and this night air begins to

Edward S. Ellis

feel chilly. It can't be far from midnight."

"I am willing; where's Terror? Ah! here he is; old fellow, come along and keep faithful watch over your friends."

"Boys," said Tim O'Rooney, with a strange, husky intonation, "you remember my dream about this steamer burning?"

"Yes; what of it?"

"It is coming thrue!"

*He spoke the truth!*

# CHAPTER III

## AFLOAT

As Tim O'Rooney spoke, he pointed to the bow of the steamer, where, in the bright moonlight, some smoke could be seen rising—where, too, the next instant, they caught sight of a gleam of fire.

"Oh, heaven! what shall we do?" exclaimed Elwood, struck with a panic.

"Wait and trust to Providence."

"Let us jump overboard; I'd rather be drowned than burned to death. Come, Howard, let's jump over this minute!"

He made a move toward the stern of the steamer, near which they had been seated, as if he intended to spring overboard, when his arm was sternly caught by the Irishman, who said in an indignant tone:

"Kaap cool! kaap cool! don't make a fool of yoursilf. Can ye swim?"

"Yes," answered Howard, "we can both swim very well. Can you?"

Edward S. Ellis

"Indaad, I can—swim like a stone."

"But good heavens!" exclaimed Elwood, who had not entirely recovered from his excitement, "the land is miles off, and we can't swim there, not taking into account the heavy sea."

"What does that mean?"

As Howard spoke, the bow of the steamer made a sweeping bend to the right.

"They've headed toward shore," said Elwood.

This snatch of conversation had occupied the shortest possible space of time. The fire had been discovered by the officials on board fully as soon as by our friends, and the men could be seen running hurriedly to and fro, all quiet and still, for they knew too well what the result would be if the alarm was communicated to the sleeping passengers. The pilot had headed the vast craft toward land, and by the furious throbbing of the engines it could be seen that the doomed vessel was straining to the utmost, like some affrighted, faithful horse striving to carry his master as nearly as possible to the port of safely ere he dropped down and died.

It was fully midnight, and, as a matter of course, very nearly all the passengers were in their berths. There were a few, however, who were lingering on the promenade deck, some smoking—here and there a couple of lovers all unconscious of everything else—one or two avaricious speculators; and but a few minutes could elapse before the startling danger should become known.

The last words, which we have given as spoken by our

friends, had scarcely been said, when a man, who apparently had been stretched out sound asleep, suddenly sprung up, wild with terror. "The boat is on fire! *fire! fire!*"

He darted hither and thither like some wild animal compassed on every hand by death, and then suddenly made a leap overboard, and was swallowed up in the sea.

The alarm spread with fearful rapidity, and was soon ringing through every part of the steamer, and now began that fearful confusion and panic which no pen can clearly picture, and which, once seen, can never be forgotten to the dying day.

Our three friends were gathered at the stern of the steamer, earnestly and anxiously discussing the best course to pursue.

"Let's stay here," said Howard, "for every second is taking us nearer land."

"That is what nearly all will do," said Elwood, "but we can never reach the shore, and when the time comes we shall all be in the sea together, struggling and sinking, and we shall then be sure to go down."

"Yez are right," said Tim, addressing the last speaker. "Our only chance is to jump overboard this very minute, before the sea is full of the poor fellows. They'll begin to go over the ship's side and will kaap it up until the thing is burned up."

"It's time then that we hunted our life-preservers," said Howard.

"Git out wid yer life-presarvers!" impatiently exclaimed Tim. "Didn't me uncle wear one of 'em for six months, and then die with the faver! I'll heave over one of these settaas, and that'll kaap up afloat."

Edward S. Ellis

"Be quick about it, Tim," urged Elwood, who was beginning to get nervous. "See, the fire is spreading, and everybody seems to have found out what the matter is."

There was indeed no time to be lost. The steamer was doomed beyond all possibility of salvation, and must soon become unmanageable, when everything would be turned into a pandemonium. One of the large settees was wrenched loose and lifted over the stern of the steamer.

"Now," said Tim, "the minute it goes over yez must follow. The owld staamer is going like a straak of lightning, and if aither of yez wait, he'll be lift behind."

"All right, no danger, go ahead!"

They now clambered up, and sat poised on the stern. In this fearful position Tim O'Rooney held the settee balanced for a few minutes.

"Be yez riddy?"

"Yes."

"Do yez jump a little to the right, Elwood, and yez a little to the left, Howard, so as not to hit the owld thing. All riddy; here we go!"

The next moment the three were spinning down through the air, and struck the water. They went below the surface, the boys sinking quite a distance; but almost instantly they arose and struck bravely out.

"Tim, where are you?" called out Elwood, not seeing his friend.

"Here, to the left," responded the Irishman, as he rose on a huge swell. "Can ye swim to me?"

"I hope so, but my clothes bother me like creation."

Strange! that not one of the three had once thought of removing their superfluous clothing before jumping into the ocean. But Elwood was a fine swimmer, and he struggled bravely, although at a great disadvantage, until his outstretched hand was seized by the Irishman, and he then caught hold of the settee and rested himself.

"Where is Howard?" he asked, panting from his exertions.

"Here he is," responded Howard himself. "I struck the water so close that when I came up my hand hit the settee."

"I tell you what it is," said Elwood. "We ought to have brought something else with us beside this. We have got to keep all of our bodies underwater for this to bear us."

"And what of it?"

"Suppose some poor fellow claims a part. Gracious! here comes a man this minute!"

"We can't turn him off," said Tim, "but this owld horse has all the grist he can carry."

A dark body could be seen struggling and rapidly approaching them.

"Whoever he is, he is a good swimmer," remarked Howard, watching the stranger.

"Of course he is, for it comes natural; don't you see it isn't a man, but old Terror."

"Thank heaven for that! we never thought about him. I am glad he is with us."

The next moment the Newfoundland placed his paw on the settee and gave a low bark to announce his joy at being among his friends. The sagacious brute seemed to understand how frail the tenure was that held them all suspended over eternity; for he did nothing more than rest the top of his paw on the precious raft.

# CHAPTER IV

## A PASSENGER

By this time our friends were a quarter of a mile in the rear of the burning steamer. The furious pulsations of the engines had stopped, and from stern to stern the great ship was one mass of soothing flame. The light threw a glare upon the clouds above, and made it so bright where our friends were floating in the water that they could have read the pages of a printed book. The illumination must have been seen for many and many a mile in every direction upon the Pacific.

"Yes, the steamer has stopped," said Howard; "the fire has reached the engines, and now they must do as we have done."

"But they have boats and may escape."

"Not half enough of them; and then what they have got will be seized by the crew, as they always do at such times."

"Look! you can see them jumping over. The poor wretches hang fast till they are so scorched that they have to let go."

"It's mighty lucky yees are here," said Tim, "for every mother's son that can swim will be hugged by a half-dozen that can't, which would be bad for me."

"Why so; can't you swim?"

"Not a bit of it."

"And nothing but this bench to keep us from sinking."

"And be the same towken isn't that good enough, if it only kaaps us afloat? Can't ye be satisfied?"

"Look! how grand!"

It was indeed a fearful sight, the steamer being one pyramid of roaring, blazing fire, sweeping upward in great fan-like rifts, then blowing outward, horizontally across the deep, as if greedy for the poor beings who had sprung in agony from its embrace. Millions of sparks were floating and drifting overhead and falling all around. The shrieks of the despairing passengers, as with their clothes all aflame they sprung blindly into the ocean, could be heard by our friends, and must indeed have extended a far greater distance.

For an hour the conflagration raged with apparently unabated violence, the wreck drifting quite rapidly; but the fire soon tired of its work, large pieces of burning timber could be seen floating in the water, and finally the charred hull made a plunge downward into the sea, and our friends were left alone upon their frail support.

"Now, it's time to decide what we are going to do," said Howard.

"You are right, and what shall it be? Shall we drift about here until morning, when some vessel will pick us up? I have no doubt this fire has drawn a half-dozen toward it."

"No; let's make for shore."

"That is the best plan," said Tim.

"But it is a good way off," remarked Howard; "and I have little hope of reaching it."

"Never mind; it, will keep us busy, and that will make the time pass faster than if we do nothing but float."

"We may need our strength; but it is the best plan."

"But do we know the direction?"

"I can tell you that," said Elwood; "for the moon was directly over the shore; so all we've got to do is to aim for the moon."

"Begorrah! we can walk and talk, as the owld lady said when her husband stopped on the way to the gallows to bid her good-by. So paddle away!"

It being a warm summer night, the water was quite pleasant, although our friends were sure to get enough of it long before they could hope to place their feet upon the earth. Having now an object, they began working with a will, the boys swimming as lustily as possible straight for the shore, while Tim assisted materially in pushing forward the craft.

The intelligent Newfoundland appeared to comprehend what was wanted, and contributed not a little to the momentum.

"Do you think we are making any progress—"

"O, save me! save me! I'm drowning!"

The voice sounded close by them, and caused an involuntary

start from all three.

"Where is he?" asked Howard, in a terrified whisper.

"There!"

At that moment they caught sight of a man fiercely buffeting the waves, as he rose on an immense swell, and then sunk down again in the trough of the sea.

"Can we do anything for him?" asked Elwood. "It's too bad to see the poor fellow sink when we may save him."

"I'm afeared the owld bench won't bear another hand on it."

But Terror had heard that cry and anticipated the wishes of his friends. Leaving them with their raft, he struck powerfully out toward the drowning man, and they both went down in the vast sea chasm together. When they came in view again upon the crest of the swell, the Newfoundland had the hair of the man's head in his teeth and had begun his return. A moment later the gasping man threw out his hands and caught the settee with such eagerness that it instantly sunk.

"Be careful!" admonished Howard, "or you'll drown us all. One of us can't swim!"

"Won't your raft bear us?"

"Yes, if you keep only your head above water and bear very lightly upon it. Don't attempt to rise up."

"All right!"

The buoyant raft came to the surface, and was instantly

grasped firmly but carefully by all. Poor Tim O'Rooney had come very near drowning. A man when suddenly cast into the water for the first time has been known to swim long and well; and the Irishman, by the most furious effort, had saved himself from strangling and sinking, although he had swallowed a good deal of the nauseating sea-water, and was now ejecting it.

"Worrah! I took an overdose that time, and it wouldn't sthay on my stomach!" he said. "I'm thinking there'll be no necessity of me swallowing any salts for some time to coom, be the towken that I've enough to last me me life-time."

"We are all right now!" said the stranger. "I can swim, but I was just about used up when your dog took me in tow. May I inquire who my friends are?"

Howard gave their names and destination, and he instantly said:

"My name is Manuel Yard, and my place of business is next door to that of your fathers."

"You know them then."

"I have known them both very well for years, and now that you have given me your names I remember you both."

After a few more words, our friends recognized him as a tall, pale-looking man, with whom they had exchanged greetings more than once on their passage from Panama.

"I've been down to the Isthmus," he added, "and was on my way home when the steamer took fire."

"Where were you when you heard the alarm?"

"Sound asleep in my berth; I had no time even to put on my clothes; but, thank God, if I can escape in any way."

"Stick to us, and help shove this craft, and I'm in hopes we'll fetch up somewhere by morning."

# CHAPTER V

## LAND

Under the united propulsion of three men and a large Newfoundland dog, the small raft moved shoreward with no insignificant speed. It was found amply sufficient to preserve them all from drowning had none known how to swim, provided they managed the matter prudently. There is so little difference in the quantity of water and the human body, that a slight effort, if properly made, will keep it afloat. The trouble with new beginners is that when they first go beyond their depth their blind struggles tend to carry them downward more than upward.

"This is rather pleasant," remarked Mr. Yard. "There is little doubt, I think, of reaching land. There is only one thing that makes the shivers run over me."

"What is that?"

"The thought of *sharks*!"

"Ugh! Why did you spake of them?" asked Tim, with a strong expression of disgust. "I've been thinking of 'em ever since I've been in the water, but I didn't want to skeer the boys."

Edward S. Ellis

"They never once entered my head," said Howard.

"Nor mine either," added Elwood. "Are they in this part of the ocean?"

"You will find them in almost every part of the sea, I was going to say. They abound off the coast of California."

"But it is night, and they will not be apt to see!"

"This fire and the numbers of drowning people will draw hundreds of the finny inhabitants toward us. You know a fire at night is sure to attract fish."

"You seem determined to frighten us," said Howard, "but I shall continue to think that God who has so mercifully saved us intends to save us to the end."

"Perhaps so, too, but it does no harm to understand all the dangers to which we are subject."

"I believe with Howard," said Elwood. "I ain't afraid of sharks, but for all that, they are ugly creatures. They swim under you and the first thing you know clip goes one of your legs off, just the same as a pair of snuffers would clip off a piece of wick."

"They are the hyenas of the sea," said Howard, "although I believe some kinds are stupid and harmless. I think I have heard them called that by somebody, I don't remember who. They will snap up anything that is thrown to them."

"Wouldn't it make their eyes water to come this way then? Jis' to think of their saaing four pair of legs dancing over their hids, not to spake of the dog that could come in by way of dessart."

"O Tim! keep still, it is too dreadful!"

"Worrah! it wasn't meself that introduced the subject, but as yez have got started, I've no objection to continue the same."

"Let us try and talk about something more pleasant—"

"A shark! a shark!" suddenly screamed Elwood, springing half his length out of the water in his excitement.

"Where?" demanded Mr. Yard, while the others were speechless with terror.

"He has hold of my leg! O, save me, for he is pulling me under!"

There was danger for a moment that all would go to the bottom, but Mr. Yard displayed a remarkable coolness that saved them all.

"It is not a shark," said he, "or he would have had your leg off before this."

"What is it then? What can it be?"

"It is a drowning man that has caught your foot as he was going down. You must kick him off or he will drown you. Has he one foot or both?"

"My left ankle is grasped by something."

"That is good; if he had hold of both feet it would be bad for you. Use your free foot and force his grasp loose."

Elwood did so with such vigor that he soon had the inexpressible relief of announcing that the drag weight was loosed and his limbs were free again.

"That is terrible," said he, as they resumed their progress. "Just to think of being seized in that way by some poor fellow who, I don't suppose, really knew what he was doing."

"How came he there?" asked Howard.

"You see, we ain't far from where the steamer sunk, and there may be more near us. This man has gone down just as we were passing by him, and in his blind struggles has caught your ankle."

"If a drowning man will catch at a straw, wouldn't he be after catching at a leg?" inquired Tim.

"It seems natural that he should do so; but we are in the most dangerous place we could be. Let's keep a sharp lookout."

Our friends peered in every direction, as they rose and sunk on the long, heaving swell of the sea. They saw pieces of charred wood and fragments of the wreck, but caught sight of no human being until Mr. Yard pointed, to a dark mass some distance away.

"That is a raft covered with people," said he.

"They seem to be standing still."

"Yes, they merely want to keep afloat until morning, when no doubt they will be picked up and cared for. Keep quiet, for if we talk too loud some one may start for us."

"And work hard," whispered Tim, struggling harder than ever. "Aich of yees shove like a locomotive."

"Good advice," added Mr. Yard, in the same cautious undertone. "Let's get away as fast as possible."

Hour after hour the men toiled, following the moon, that appeared to recede from them as they advanced. They had passed safely the debris of the wrecked steamer, and were again talking loudly and rather cheerfully, when Tim O'Rooney interrupted them:

"Yonder is something flowting in the darkness."

"It is a boat full of people," said Mr. Yard. "I have noticed it for the last few minutes."

All turned their eyes toward the spot indicated, and agreed that Mr. Yard was correct in his supposition.

"I will hail it," he quietly added, and then called out: "Boat ahoy!"

"What do you want?" came back in a gruff voice.

"Can you take four drowning passengers on board?"

"Not much," was the unfeeling answer, "Paddle away and you'll reach California one of these days."

"How far are we from it?"

"Double the distance, divide by two, and you'll have it."

Nothing further was extracted from the men, but they could be heard laughing and talking boisterously with each other, and the odor of their pipes was plainly detected, so close were the parties.

"Thank heaven, we are not dependent upon them!" said Mr. Yard. "If we were, we should fare cruelly indeed."

"Who are they?"

"A part of the crew of the steamer, who seized the boat at the first appearance of danger, and left the helpless to perish."

An hour later, long after the boat had disappeared, and when our friends were toiling bravely forward, a low, dark object directly in front attracted their notice.

"What is it?" whispered Elwood.

"*It is land!*" was the joyful reply. "I am walking upon the sand this minute, and you can do the same!"

# CHAPTER VI

## THE CALIFORNIA COAST

They were safe at last! The four dropped their feet and found them resting upon smooth packed sand, and wading a few rods they all stood upon dry earth. Terror, as he shook his shaggy coat and rubbed his nose against his young masters seemed not the least joyful of the party.

"Isn't this grand!" exclaimed Elwood. "When did the ground feel better to your feet? Saved from fire and water!"

"Our first duty is to thank God!" said Mr. Yard reverently. "He has chosen us out of the hundreds that have perished as special objects of his mercy. Let us kneel upon the shore and testify our gratitude to Him."

All sunk devoutly upon their knees and joined the merchant, as in a low, impressive tone he returned thanks to his Creator for the signal mercy he had displayed in bringing them safely through such imminent perils.

"Now, what is to be done next?" inquired Mr. Yard, as they arose to their feet and looked around them. "The first thing I should like to do is to procure a suit of clothes, and I hope I shall be able to do it without stripping any of the dead bodies

Edward S. Ellis

that will soon wash ashore."

"What is the naad?" asked Tim O'Rooney. "Baing that it's a warrum summer night, and there saams to be few in the neighborhood that is likely to take exsaptions to your costume."

"But day is breaking!" replied the merchant, pointing across the low, rocky country to a range of mountains in the distance, whose high, jagged tops were blackly defined against the sky that was growing light and rosy behind them.

"Yes, it will soon be light," said Howard. "See! there are persons along the shore that have come down to the wreck?"

"They are some of the passengers that have managed to reach land. I will go among them and see whether any of them have any clothing to sell," laughed Mr. Yard as he moved away.

As the sun came up over the mountains it lit up a dreary and desolate scene. Away in the distance, until sky and earth mingled into one, stretched the blue Pacific, not ridged into foam and spray like the boisterous Atlantic, but swelling and heaving as if the great deep was a breathing monster. A few fragments of blackened splinters floating here and there were all that remained to show where a few hours before the magnificent steamer, surcharged with its living freight, so proudly cut the waters on her swift course toward the Golden Gate.

Several ghastly, blue-lipped survivors in their clinging garments were wandering aimlessly along the shore, the veriest pictures of utter misery, as they mumbled a few words to each other, or stared absently around. They seemed to be partially bereft of their senses, and were probably somewhat dazed from the fearful scenes through which they had so recently passed.

Several sails were visible, but they were so far away that it was vain to hope to attract their attention. Three large boats could be seen away to the northwest, skirting along shore and making their way toward San Francisco as rapidly as muscle and oars could carry them. What recked they whether the passengers were buried with the steamer, sunk in the ocean, or left to perish on the desolate coast?

The Coast Range, which descends into California from Oregon, in some places comes within twenty-five or thirty miles of the sea, while at other times it recedes to over a hundred. The particular point where our friends were suffered to land was rough, barren and rocky, and behind them, with many peaks reaching the line of perpetual snow, rose the noble Coast Range, between which and them stretched a smaller range of mountains.

Around them the country appeared desolate and uninhabited. Howard and Elwood were well acquainted with geography, and had a general idea of California, although they could not be expected to know much of the minor facts of the State. They were aware that at no great distance—but whether north or south it was impossible to say—lay the missionary town of San Luis Obispo, and between them and the Coast Range ran the Salinas River, formerly known as the San Buenaventura, and a smaller chain of mountains or highlands.

They knew, too, that after crossing the Coast Range, you descended into the broad and beautiful Sacramento Valley, where abounded wild animals, Indians, gold, silver, and the most exuberant vegetation. This was about all they knew; and this, after all, was considerable. When persons expect to

Edward S. Ellis

make a journey to some distant country they are very apt to learn all that they possibly can about it; and this was the way they came to understand so much regarding the young State of California.

They had stood some little time conversing together when they saw Mr. Yard approaching, clad in quite a respectable suit of black, albeit, as a matter of course, it was thoroughly soaked with salt water.

"You are fortunate," remarked Howard.

"Yes," he laughed; "what strange beings we are! Do you see that elderly gentleman yonder, with his hands in his pockets walking back and forth as though he expected some arrival from the sea?"

The personage alluded to could be easily distinguished from the others.

"Well, his berth was next to mine. When the alarm of fire was first heard he sprung from his bed, dressed himself and caught up his valise, which contained an extra suit of clothing, and rushed on deck with the other passengers."

"How was he saved?"

"It is hard to tell. He and several others hung fast to some such sort of a raft as we had, and managed to get ashore. And all the time he grasped that valise, even when besought by his companions to let it go, find when it endangered his chances of life fully ten-fold."

"He must be very poor."

"Poor! He is worth half a million in gold this minute. That

valise contained all his property that he had entrusted to the steamer, and it was his fear that he might lose the few dollars that it is worth that made him cling so tenaciously to it."

"How was it that he gave them to you?"

"No fear that he gave them. I stated in the presence of two witnesses that, I would give him a hundred dollars for the suit as soon as we reached San Francisco. He racked his brains to see whether there was not some means of my giving him my note for the amount; but as that couldn't be done under the circumstances, he did the next best thing and established my obligation in the mouth of several witnesses."

"Strange man! But, Mr. Yard, what is to be done?"

"I intend to wait here during the day, as I know of nothing better that we can do. I think some friends will find us before nightfall."

"We have decided to go inland a short distance, dry our clothes and give our bodies a good rubbing, to prevent our taking cold."

"A wise precaution, but useless in my case as I have already caught a very severe one."

"Should we become separated, you will tell our parents that we reached the land in safety and are in good spirits."

"Of course; but don't wander too far away, as you may lose your chance of being taken off. You know this isn't the most hospitable country in the world. There are treacherous and thieving Indians in these parts, and they would have swooped down on us long ago if they had only known we were here. As it is, I fear their approach before a friendly sail comes to us."

"Never fear; we will take good care not to wander too far away."

And the parties separated for a much longer time than any of them imagined.

# CHAPTER VII

## THE RESCUE

Our three friends—although it seems equally proper to speak of four, as Terror was a most important member of the party—walked away from the sea-shore and began making their way back into the country. As we have hinted in another place, they found this section wild and desolate. Little else than huge rocks, bowlders and stunted trees met the eye, while there was no appearance of vegetation, nor was the slightest vestige of a human habitation visible, let them look in whatever direction they chose.

The air was clear, the sky decked by a few fleecy clouds over the Pacific, and there was little doubt that the day would be a fine, warm one. The climate of California is mild, except when the winds from the Pacific bring chilling fogs along the coast. The view in the east was particularly grand, the peaks of the gigantic Coast mountains and of the smaller range rising and swelling in vast peaks, appearing as if the Pacific when tossed and driven by some hurricane had suddenly congealed with the foam upon the tops of its mountainous billows. Looking northward, the last object that met the eye was these mountains gradually blending with the brilliant sky, while to the southward the prospect was repeated.

Edward S. Ellis

They wandered along, springing up the sides of rocks, jumping quite a distance to the ground, again passing around those that were too high to climb, Terror all the time frolicking at their sides, certainly as happy as any of them, while they chatted and laughed, their hearts buoyant in the beautiful summer and the pleasing retrospect of a thrilling adventure already safely passed through and the prospect of a few others close at hand.

In this wandering manner they at last found themselves fully a mile from shore, and in a wild, rocky place where they felt secure from observation. Here all removed their clothes, subjected their bodies to a vigorous rubbing that made the surface glow with warmth and reaction, and then spread their garments out to dry. Their extended walk before reaching this place had partially done the latter for them, so that in the course of an hour or so they found them free from all moisture, and as they donned them they once more felt like themselves.

"Now," said Elwood, "I am very tired and sleepy; is not this a good place to lie down and rest?"

"I was going to suggest the same thing," added Howard. "I do not see in what better manner we can spend a few hours."

"And it's the same idaa that has been strhiking me ever since we sot foot in this qua'r looking place. It's meself that is so sleapy that at ivery wink I makes I has to lift the eyelids up with my fingers, and me eyes feels as though the wind has been blowing sand in 'em all day."

The proposal thus being satisfactory to all, they proceeded to carry it out at once. The day was so mild that the only precaution necessary was to secure themselves against the rays of the sun. This was easily done, and stretching out beneath the shelter of a projecting ledge of rocks they had scarcely laid down when all were sound asleep.

And leaving them here for the time being, we give our attention for a few moments to the survivors of the steamer.

Some thirty odd of the passengers succeeded in reaching the shore, while about a dozen were saved with the crew, who, as is generally the case at such times, acted upon the idea that it was their duty to take charge of the boats and prevent the passengers from risking themselves in such frail structures. After all, no doubt their lives were as valuable as were those of the hundreds they carried, and their conduct, when viewed in an unprejudiced manner, perhaps was not so criminal.

The destruction of so large a steamer along the California coast, in the regular track of the vessels going to and coming from Panama, could not occur without the knowledge of many upon the ocean. Indeed, the glare upon the heavens was seen far up the coast, and in San Luis Obispo, to the south, was pronounced by all to be caused by the burning of some large vessel at sea.

It so came about that there were but two vessels near enough to go to the relief of the unfortunate steamer; but these were controlled by rival captains, each of whom hoped to enter the Golden Gate an hour or so in advance of the other; and therefore they had not time to slacken sail and lay to, but pressed forward with an expression of regret that the necessities of the case compelled them thus to refuse all succor to the needy ones.

But there were others at a greater distance who bore down upon the fiery scene at once; but they were miles away when the last vestige of the steamer disappeared, and it was only a matter of conjecture as to where a few of the survivors might be struggling with the waves. Not until the sun had been up over an hour did the man at the mast-head of the nearest vessel call out that he saw several boats pulling up the coast, while a few persons could be seen on the shore making signals to attract their attention.

Some time after, the Relief—happily named—cast anchor a half-mile from land and two boats put off from her side. The survivors were quickly within them, and they were about putting off again when the mate of the Relief said:

"Are you all here?"

"Yes, yes," was the impatient reply of Mr. Tiflings, the man who had sold the suit of clothes to Mr. Yard, "don't wait any longer. I shall lose $500 by not being in San Francisco to-day."

"But they are not all here," interrupted Mr. Yard, in some excitement. "There are two boys in charge of an Irishman that are missing."

"Where are they?" asked the mate.

"They went back from the shore some time ago. I do not think they can be at any great distance."

"Perhaps if you called to them they might hear you."

Mr. Yard sprung out upon the beach, ran to and mounted a goodly-sized rock, and shouted at the top of his voice. He called again and again, and listened intently, but there was no response.

All this time Mr. Tiflings sat leaning his head forward and nervously beating a tattoo upon the side of the boat with his long, thin fingers. Occasionally he glanced at the "foolish" Mr. Yard, and muttered:

"What nonsense! What valuable time we are losing by his childishness! Time is too precious to fritter away in this manner!"

While the kind-hearted merchant was shouting himself hoarse, our friends were heavily and sweetly slumbering, totally oblivious to external things, as indeed they would have been were he within a few rods of them, instead of over a mile away. Finally he was compelled to give up the task and reluctantly return to the boat.

"This is too bad," said he, "to leave them in this manner. What will become of them?"

"They will be picked up by some of the passing vessels."

"Certainly, certainly," assented Mr. Tiflings, "don't wait any longer; it will be a week before we get into San Francisco."

"We will row away," said the mate, "and if we see anything of them before we reach the vessel we will put back and take them aboard."

This was reasonable, and Mr. Yard could not object to it. The sailors plied their oars, and the passengers were borne swiftly toward the friendly Relief. Mr. Yard kept his eyes fixed upon the bleak coast which they were so rapidly leaving behind them. He saw nothing of his friends; but, after reaching the ship's deck, he took the spy-glass from the captain and discovered a party of a dozen Indians wandering up and down the beach as if in quest of plunder. Finally, sail was hoisted, the Relief bore away to the northward, and the scene of the rescue dwindled away and vanished in the distance.

Edward S. Ellis

# CHAPTER VIII

## INDIANS

The sleep of perfect health is dreamless, and is not easily aroused by external disturbance. Tim O'Rooney, Elwood Brandon and Howard Lawrence, sweetly forgetful of the need of their being within sight and hearing of the shore, slept through the entire day without once awaking. The sun was just dipping beneath the Pacific when Howard opened his eyes with that confused, indistinct recollection which often takes possession of our faculties when first aroused from a deep slumber. He stared around and the sight of the unconscious forms of his two companions, and the mute Newfoundland dog with his nose between his paws, but blinking as if to show he "slept with one eye open," quickly recalled his situation. In considerable alarm, he sprung up, and began rousing the others. As they rubbed their eyes and rose to the sitting position, he said in excitement:

"Do you know we have slept ever since morning?"

"It can't be possible!" exclaimed Elwood.

"I should say we had slept a waak be the token of the hunger I feels," said Tim, with a most woeful countenance.

"I don't see any likelihood of our getting anything to digest in these parts," replied Howard.

"And where else shall we look for the same?"

"Nowhere that I know of."

"Suppose some ship has stopped here while we have been asleep!" suddenly interrupted Elwood.

"Wouldn't they have looked for us? But then they couldn't have known where we were," said Howard, asking and answering his own question in the same breath.

"We are in a pretty fix then," was the comment of Elwood, laughing at the doleful countenances he saw.

"Boys," said Tim, hitching up his pantaloons and scratching his head, "shall I tell yees something to your advantage, as the papers say?"

"Of course," answered Howard, "nothing could suit us better."

"Well, then, while we've been slaaping, our friends along shore have been carried away, and we're lift to make ourselves comfortable, as the peddler said when he hung himself up by his foot."

"Let us see!" exclaimed Elwood, "perhaps we are not too late yet."

The three rushed ever the rocks pell-mell, the dog being at their side, and giving vent now and then to short, sharp barks, as if he enjoyed the ramble.

Elwood was at the head, and had run but a short distance when he sprung upon a bowlder higher than the others, and shading his eyes for a moment as he looked off toward the sea, he called back:

"Yes, yonder they are! We are not left alone."

"But it's good to have company!" laughed Tim, "it won't be long before some vessel will step in and lift us aboard."

"How odd they look!" remarked Elwood, as his friends clambered up beside him. "They don't seem dressed in their usual fashion."

The Irishman, upon rising to his feet on top of the rock, uttered an expression of surprise, looked intently toward the sea, and then quickly sprung back again.

"Off of there quick!" he commanded in a hoarse whisper, at the same time catching the shoulder of the up-climbing Howard and forcing him back again.

"Why, what's the matter?" asked Elwood, a vague alarm taking possession of him, as he rather hurriedly obeyed him.

"May the good Lord presarve us! *them are Injuns!*"

"I thought they looked odd," said Elwood, "but I did not think of that. Are they friendly?"

"Friendly!" repeated Tim, with an expression of intense disgust. "Do you know what they are walking up and down the sand fur in that sassy shtyle?"

"Plunder, I suppose."

"Yis; they are in hopes the saa may wash up some poor fellow that they may have the pleasure of hacking him to pieces."

"Are they such terrible creatures. Perhaps they have slain those who escaped from the steamer."

"Niver a fear; there was too many of 'em, as me brother used to say when his wife tuk her broomstick at him."

"But they had no weapons to use."

Tim shook his head. He evidently had a small opinion of the courage of the California aborigines.

"Had they massacred the survivors, we could see their bodies along shore," remarked Howard. "The sun throws such a glare upon the sand that we can detect a very small object."

This settled the matter in the mind of Elwood, who had been heartsick at the great fear of such a fate having befallen his friends.

"Then the burning of the steamer has attracted the notice of a great many vessels, and I think Mr. Yard was right when he was sure of being taken off by some one."

"What a mistake we made in wandering away and going to sleep where no one could find us!"

"We did, indeed, Elwood; we voluntarily banished ourselves."

"But Mr. Yard certainly knows we are here, and will he not get a company of men to come after us?"

"Perhaps so; but, if he doesn't, your father and mine will

certainly do so, so soon as they find where we are."

"Yes, but what is to become of us between to-night and that time? I am half-starved to death, and must get something to eat pretty soon."

"Providence, that has preserved us so kindly thus far, will still watch over us."

"There's one bad thing," remarked Tim, "them Injins will hang around the shore, and it won't do for us to show ourselves niver a bit."

The faces of the two boys now blanched with fear, for they understood the danger that threatened them. It was truly a fear-inspiring sight, as they gazed out from their hiding-place in the direction of the sea. The sun was partially down the horizon, and appeared unnaturally large, while the gaunt Indians, in their fantastic costume, assumed the form of giants striding along apparently on the gleaming surface of the ocean itself. They were outlined with that sharp, black distinctness which is seen when at night a fireman runs along the outer walls of a burning building.

"Just to think!" said Elwood "we haven't a gun or a pistol with us."

"And I'm a little hungry, as the man said after fasting three waaks."

"Suppose they saw you?" said Howard.

"I ain't sure but what they did. They are looking in this direction, and appear to be disputing about some matter."

There were grounds for this alarming view of the case. The

Indians numbered about a dozen, and half of these could be seen in a knot, gesticulating in their extravagant manner, while the others were running up and down the shore as if they had detected something interesting in the surf.

"Are they looking at us?"

"There is such a glare, from the sun that I cannot tell whether their faces or backs are toward us. Tim, what do you say?"

The Irishman gazed long and carefully over the face of the rock, and finally said:

"They've seen something this way that has tuk their eye."

"They are moving, too."

"Maybe they've seen the dog, and are coming to look for us."

"Heaven save us!" exclaimed Tim, in some excitement, "there's no maybe about it; they're coming, sure!"

# CHAPTER IX

## THE PURSUIT

It was not the first time that Tim O'Rooney made a mistake. The Indians were excited over something, but as yet they held no suspicion that three white persons stood behind them and could be so easily reached. They were talking in a wild manner, and ran several rods from the beach, when they suddenly paused and picked up an object over which they quarreled and were almost ready to proceed to violence. From where our friends stood it looked as if it were nothing more than a coat or some cast-off garment that had been thrown aside by so me of the survivors when they were taken away by the Relief.

"No, they have not seen us yet," said Howard, who was watching them intently, while his two companions where looking upon the readiest means of escape.

"Then why did they start after us, be the same token?" demanded Tim, with a great sigh of relief.

"They are quarreling over something that lies upon the beach."

"If they'd only have the onspakable kindness to go to fighting each other like a lot of Kilkenny cats, and not sthop till there's not one of 'em left—I say if they'd have the kindness to do that, it would be fortinit for us."

"Hardly probable, Tim; the fact, is they appear to have settled the matter already, and have gone down to the edge of the sea again."

"I don't see the use of our remaining here," said Howard. "We daren't go any nearer them than we now are, while if we put back into the country we stand a chance of getting something to eat. As near as I can calculate, the Salinas River isn't very far away, and California is said to be very fertile along its streams, if it is barren in such places as this."

"And we may come upon a party of miners further inland."

"I don't know about that," rejoined Howard. "The diggings are on the other side of the Coast Range, between that and the Sierra Nevada, in the Sacramento Valley, and I think they are further north, too."

"Let's lave," said Tim; "if we only start tramping perhaps I may git my mind off the subject and forgit that I'm hungry enough to eat a toad, which I'd starve to death afore I'd do the same."

While they were thus debating with themselves, Terror, unobserved by any of them, whisked to the top of a high rock and announced his discovery of the Indians by several loud, gruff barks. At so great a distance it was impossible that the dog should be heard, but the danger was that the lynx-eyed savages would see him, and thus discover the presence of his friends. The peril was imminent, and a hasty word from Howard brought the Newfoundland to their feet.

But it was too late. He had scarcely ascended his perch when an Indian caught sight of him, and giving out a strange half-whoop and stream, he started on a full run toward him, closely followed by half of the entire party.

"There's no mistake this time!" exclaimed Howard, wheeling round and springing away. "Don't wait."

There was no waiting by either Tim or Elwood. The two boys were slim and fleet-footed, and could easily distance their more awkward companion; but they could not leave him alone, although he besought them to secure their own safety, while he would attend to his.

There were several things in favor of the fugitives and several against them. It was growing dark quite rapidly, and they had a good start; but the pursuers ran over the rocks and bowlders with the facility of mountain goats and gained very rapidly; they were also familiar with the face of the country, while our friends were literally "going blind."

"But don't we make 'em run!" called out Tim, glancing over his shoulder. "Them fellers was made to travel, and if they'd only throw down their guns and take up a sprig of the shillaleh, like an ilegant gintleman should do, I wouldn't ax better fun than to jine in wid 'em and tach 'em a few scientific tricks, such as can be got in Tipperary and nowhere ilse—Worrah!—"

Tim's exclamation was caused by catching his foot against a large stone and falling flat upon his face with considerable violence. He quickly scrambled up again, while Elwood anxiously inquired whether he was hurt by the fall.

"Not by the fall, plase your honor, but by the stone that whacked me betwaan the eyes."

"They are gaining!" whispered Howard, pausing a moment for his companions to come up.

"Yes, but it will be so dark in a few minutes that they can't see us, and then we will hide ourselves until the danger is past. Let us get along an fast as possible while the danger lasts."

They did strain themselves to the utmost, and speedily reached a more open country, where they could travel with greater safety. This, which at first appeared sadly against their prospects, was really the means of securing their escape. The moment they reached it they darted away at almost double their rate of speed, and shortly reached another hilly portion, into which they plunged, and running a short distance, at a signal from Howard, they dropped flat upon their faces, and crawled beneath thy sheltering projections of the rocks, Terror at the same time nestling down by the prostrate form of Elwood.

In a few minutes they heard the tramp of their swift-footed pursuers, who were running without exchanging words with each other, or uttering those exultant whoops which the Indian of other portions of our country are so accustomed to give when exulting in the certainty of capturing their enemies.

Our friends did not venture to exchange a word with each other until a long time after the Indians had passed, and nothing could be heard to indicate that they were anywhere in the neighborhood. Then they crawled near together and spoke in low whispers.

"They are gone!" said Elwood.

"I think so," replied Howard, "but they may be watching

somewhere. We must be very careful. How is it, Terror, are there any strangers near us?"

The dog snuffed the air, but made no sound, which was a negative reply.

"I guess he is right," added Howard. "We will get as far away from here as we can, for I am sure those Indians will look around here until morning in the hope of getting us then."

All three crawled a considerable ways on their hands and knees, when they stealthily arose to their feet, and seeing nothing suspicious, followed a northeasterly direction—one that would both lead them away from their pursuers and at the same time take them toward the Salinas or San Buenaventura River, which point they hoped to reach some time the next day.

After going some distance they walked more rapidly, and ventured to exchange words with each other. Terror kept the advance, fully aware of the responsibility that rested upon him. There was little fear but that he would give timely notice of the approach of danger, and a sense of comparative security took possession of our friends as they proceeded.

To their great surprise, after journeying a half-mile or so, the character of the country underwent a great change. The ground became more level, and they found themselves traveling among stunted trees and sparse vegetation. The moon did not rise until quite late, so that until then they could barely see each other's bodies as they moved along. This made them uncertain as to whether they were following the right course; but they were greatly pleased to find that they had deviated but slightly from the line they intended to pursue.

All at once a low whine from Terror arrested them. At the same instant all three detected the glimmer of a light among the trees. Cautiously approaching, Tim O'Rooney in the advance, he said in his husky whisper:

"There's an owld Injin noddin' by the fire, and if he has a gun, or anything to eat, we'll try and get him to lend 'em to us!"

# CHAPTER X

## A GOOD SAMARITAN

The three carefully approached the camp-fire, and soon assured themselves that there was but a single person near it, an old Indian who sat with closed eyes and nodding head, totally unmindful of their presence.

"Yes, he is all alone," remarked Howard, in response to the statement that Tim had made on first seeing the fire. "But he has no gun, so far as I can see."

"Has he anything to eat?" inquired Elwood. "For that is getting to be the most important matter."

"There doesn't appear to be any."

"Jist howld still where you baas, till I takes a look around," said Tim, with an admonitory wave of the hand.

They obeyed while he went still nearer on tiptoe. When he was scarcely twenty feet away he paused, and stooping down and bending his head first to one side and then to the other, and raising and arching his neck until his longitudinal dimensions became fearful, he at last satisfied himself that the Indian was alone.

Without moving his feet, Tim now turned his head and motioned for his companions to join him. They did so very carefully and silently, and the three men then stood where the light of the fire shone full in their faces, and where they could not help being the first objects the Indian would see when he was pleased to look up.

"We'll have to wake him," whispered Tim, "and shall I yill, or hit him with a stone on top of the head?"

"Neither; I have heard that the slumber of Indians is very light, and if you just speak or make a slight noise I have no doubt it will rouse him."

The fire, which had at its first kindling been large, was now smouldering as though it had not been touched for several hours. The Indian was seated on a large stone, his arms hanging listlessly over his knees, and his head sunk so low that his features could not be seen. Instead of the defiant scalp-lock drooping from his crown, his hair was long and luxuriant, and plentifully mixed with gray. It hung loosely over his shoulders, and in front of his face, and helped to give him a strange, repulsive appearance.

"I say, owld gintleman, are you draaming, or—"

As quick as lightning the head of the Indian flashed up, and his black eyes were centered with a look of alarm upon the individuals before him. Tim had had some experience with these people when a miner, and he now began making signs to the savage, who seemed on the point of springing up and darting away. Naturally enough the Irishman continued talking, although it was certain that the one could not understand a word the other uttered.

"We maan no harrum," said the Irishman, raising his hands

Edward S. Ellis

and letting them fall at his side, to show that he carried no weapons, and held good will toward the stranger. The boys judged it best to imitate their comrade; and after standing a few moments, the three walked quietly up to the fire. The startled Indian instantly rose to his feet and placed his hand upon the haft of a large knife at his waist.

"None of that, ye spalpeen, or I'll smash you to smithereens!" said Tim, who, although his words were of such dire portent, spoke as gently as if he were seeking to quiet an infant.

They now noticed that the Indian was very old. His face was scarred and wrinkled, his body bent, and his limbs tottered as if scarcely able to bear his weight; but his eye was as keen and defiant as the eagle's, and he stood ready to defend himself if harm were offered him.

Tim did the most prudent thing possible. He advanced straight to the savage and offered his hand. This means of salutation was understood by the latter, who, after some tottering hesitation, raised his right hand from the knife and returned the pressure. Dropping it, he looked toward Elwood and Howard, who saluted him in the same manner, and the parties were now satisfied regarding the feelings of each other.

"Ask him for something to eat!" said Elwood; "I am beginning to feel faint for the want of food."

"What good will the same do? He hasn't anything to give."

"He must live some way himself, and what will support such an old man as he is, is surely good for us."

The signs that Tim now made were unmistakable in their import. He opened his huge mouth until the cavern was fearful to contemplate; then he snapped his teeth together like a dog that has failed to catch a piece of meat thrown to him; after which he carried his hand back and forth to his mouth, and opened and shut it again.

The Indian watched these manuevers a moment, and then gave an exclamation intended solely for his own benefit—and which, therefore, it is not necessary to give, if we could, and we can't—and turning his back, commenced moving away with the feeble, uncertain gait of old age.

"What does that mean?" inquired Howard.

The savage, seeing they did not follow, paused and looked back.

"That is an invitation," said Tim; "do yees foller."

"But where will he lead us?"

"How can I tell?"

"But it may be into danger," admonished the most cautious Howard.

"It's the only chance we've got to save ourselves from starving, and for me getting a shmoke out of a pipe, which I am as hungry for as I am for a few pounds of mate."

The three, the Irishman taking the lead, did not hesitate longer, but stepped forward, and the Indian immediately resumed his guidance. The boys could not avoid some alarm and misgiving in thus following blindly an Indian whom they had not seen until a few minutes before, and who, they had every reason to believe, was hostile; but there seemed no other course, and they obeyed the suggestion of Tim O'Rooney.

The Indian led the way for several hundred yards, when he halted before one of the rudest and oddest habitations imaginable. It was made of stones, stumps, limbs, dirt and skins, its dimensions being about twenty feet in every direction. The savage paused but a moment when he shoved a large skin aside, entered and held it open for his friends to do the same. Tim O'Rooney peered cautiously into the lodge before trusting himself within it, but seeing nothing alarming, he stepped briskly forward, and was followed by the two boys and Terror.

A dim fire was burning in one corner, against the face of a rock, and opposite it lay a bundle of clothes, which, upon being rather roughly touched by the foot of the Indian, resolved itself into a being of the feminine gender, unquestionably the partner of the master of the lodge. A few words were exchanged between the two, when the squaw busied herself in preparing a meal, while her husband stirred the fire into a cheerful blaze that brightly illuminated every portion of the singular dwelling. He seemed entirely forgetful of the presence of the strangers, who seated themselves upon a broad flat stone and calmly awaited the result of his doings.

The old lady speedily appeared with a huge piece of meat, which was soon roasting on the fire, its savory odor filling the apartment, and rendering our friends half frantic in their starving condition. It was quickly cooked; the Indian severed it into four equal portions with his hunting-knife, and tossed one to each of his visitors, including the dog, which was really suffering for the want of nourishment.

As Elwood and Howard ravenously ate the well-cooked, juicy meat, free from pepper and salt, they were sure they had never tasted such a delicious morsel in all their life. The pieces were of a generous size, and after all three had gormandized themselves until, absolutely, they could contain no more, each had some left. This, as a matter of course, was thrown to Terror, and by the time he had swallowed them all, he licked his jaws to show that his pangs of hunger were also fully satisfied.

Edward S. Ellis

# CHAPTER XI

## FURTHER EAST

"With your lave?" said Tim O'Rooney, stepping forward and drawing the pipe of their Indian host from his mouth. The latter gazed at him in amazement but said nothing, and offered no objection to the impudent proceeding.

"I fales better," complacently added the Irishman as he emitted volume after volume of tobacco smoke. "We've had a good schlape, a good male, and I'm quieting my narves with the ould gintleman's pipe."

"It strikes me, Tim, you were rather discourteous," said Elwood. "Be careful that we do not trespass too much on his good nature."

"This is the calomel o' pace, as they calls it, and when you shmoke it it manes there's no enmity atween us. You see, the ould gintleman and meself have shmoked it together, and that makes us frinds. That is a wise shtroke of policy on the part of Tim O'Rooney, beside the comfort it gives him. Will aither of yez indulge in a few whiffs?"

Both replied that they did not use the weed in any form.

"That's right. It makes me indignant when I sees a youngster puffing away at a pipe or a segar; but never mind that, boys; do yez jist look over the top of our ould frind's head and tell me whether yez sees anything."

"I have noticed that fine-looking rifle before," replied Howard; "I only wish each of us had such a one."

"We will have that before we lave this mansion. Do ye mind that, boys?"

"I will starve to death before I will consent to take it away from the old Indian after the kind treatment he has given us," said Howard.

"So would I," promptly added Elwood. "No matter how badly we may want it I shall never consent to steal it."

"Shtale it! Who talks of shtaling it!" indignantly demanded Tim. "You're a couple of fine spalpeens, ain't you, to think that of me. I mane to buy it, and give the ould man his own price."

"What have you to buy it with?" asked Elwood in surprise. "I have a little money, but I don't believe it is enough to buy such a good-looking gun as that."

"No; if your pockets were lined with gold pieces he would care nothing for them," said Howard; "but what will you offer him, Tim?"

"Each of you has a knife, and likewise have I; you carry two pretty fine gold watches, while I've a bull's-eye as big as a half-dozen like them. An Injun will sell his squaw and lodge for such trifles."

"Well, try it, then."

The Irishman arose to his feet when, as a matter of course, the black eye of the old man was fixed upon him. He pointed to the gun overhead, whereupon the Indian, with surprising quickness, caught it down and held it with a nervous grasp, his squaw taking his seat beside him. Tim offered the three knives which the party owned for it, opening and flicking them to excite his cupidity. The eager look that came into his face showed that he understood what was meant; but he only hugged his property more tightly and shook his head from side to side.

"I knew he wouldn't part with it," said Elwood.

"Howld on a minute," replied Tim; "I'm only throwing out me skirmishers; I'll fetch him yet. He's larned how to make a bargain."

The Irishman now produced his watch—an immense affair that would have made a load for a small child. He pried open its gigantic case and showed the dazzling array of brass wheels and the glittering coil of steel. It could not but be attractive to a savage mind, and the Indian's eyes sparkled as he looked upon it.

"Keep yours and let me offer mine," said Howard.

"Howld on, I tell yees, howld on; maybe you'll both have to offer 'em afore he'll bite. My repater is like myself—it took too much salt water for its good and hasn't been well for a few months. If the ould thing would only tick a little he couldn't resist it; it has a beautiful voice when it starts—like a thrashing machine."

Equally to the surprise of Tim and the boys, the savage arose and handed the gun to the Irishman, who was only too glad to put his watch and three knives into his possession.

"I only wish he had a couple more," said Howard, "so that we could each get one. We ought to be able to take care of ourselves then."

Tim in the meantime was turning the rifle over in his hand and examining it with an appearance of great pleasure.

"That come from San Francisco," said he.

"How did it reach these parts?"

"Aisy enough, as me uncle said when he fell off the house. Some trader has let him have it for about five hundred dollars' worth of furs and peltries."

"Don't forget the ammunition," admonished Elwood, "or the gun will do us little good."

"Worrah! it's meself that came nigh doin' the same. That's a fine powdther-horn that he has. I say, Misther—"

Tim now began motioning very earnestly for this article, bullet-pouch and box of percussion caps that the savage had at his side; but the shrewd old fellow was sharper than they expected. He indulged in a peculiar grin, and held them very rigidly.

Howard laughed.

"You don't get anything more without paying for it?"

"What shall I pay? I've alriddy overdrawn me bank account, as they say."

"Let him take my watch," said Elwood. "Fact is, I think it has been ruined by the salt water."

"No, that's too much; haven't ye got some trinket about yees that isn't good for nothing and that you doesn't want?"

The boys searched themselves. Elwood finally produced a small silver pencil.

"Just the thing," said Tim.

But the old Indian, evidently failed to consider it just the thing, for he continued obdurate and shook his head.

A new idea struck Howard. He wrenched off several brass buttons from his coat, and handed them to Tim. The eyes of their host fairly sparkled, as does a child's at sight of a coveted toy, and rising to his feet he tottered hastily toward them, and tossed the coveted articles into the Irishman's lap.

"Now, if the owld gentleman would only dispose of his pipe and a ton or two of tobaccy to me, or make me a prisent of 'em, I'd lave and feel aisy."

A few more brass buttons procured this also, and our friends had good cause to feel delighted over the result of the bargain.

"There doesn't seem to be anything more that we can do, and it strikes me that it would be prudent for us to leave," said Howard.

"I think so," added Elwood. "I believe there are other Indians at hand, or within call, else he wouldn't be so willing to part with his gun."

The savage now rose and acted in rather a singular manner. Walking to the opening which answered for a door, he passed out and motioned for his visitors to follow. They did so, and when upon the outside he pointed off to the east, nodded his head, and swept his left arm.

"What does he mean?" asked Howard, totally at a loss to understand him.

"He means that this is the direction for us to follow."

"He maans, too, that there's danger in waiting here, and that we'd better be thramping."

Elwood took a step or two in the direction indicated to test the meaning of their friend. He nodded very earnestly, and satisfied them all that the safest plan was for them to leave as soon as possible, and take the course pointed out by him.

Accordingly, thanking him as well as they could by signs, the three moved away toward the east.

# CHAPTER XII

## THE SALINAS VALLEY

Our friends journeyed forward until broad daylight, when they found themselves fairly among the high range of hills which in this portion of California comes down almost to the edge of the sea. The scenery was bleak and rugged, and the country was barren and showed very few signs of vegetation, so that for all practical purposes they were little better than if in the sandy desert of the south-eastern portion of the State.

They observed, too, a disagreeable change in the climate. The moist winds of the Pacific being cooled by these mountains caused the air to become chilly and foggy and all felt the need of additional clothing.

They had now concluded to pass through these hills to the Salinas Valley and then follow this northward until they reached the more settled portion of California, or come upon a party of miners or hunters, in whose company they could feel safe against the treacherous Indians, and who might perhaps afford them their much-needed weapons and more abundant food.

The latter question assumed the first importance with them. They saw no fruits, and very few animals. The discharge of their rifle was dangerous, as it could be heard at a great distance, and if there is any creature that is extraordinarily inquisitive it is the American aborigine.

Several times they heard the faint report of guns in the distance, but for some days saw no human beings except themselves. At night, when they lay down to rest, Terror kept a more faithful watch over them than either of their number could do. They generally found some secure place among the rocks where they could slumber in safety.

On the third day after the shipwreck they crossed the dividing ridge and had a view of Salinas or San Buenaventura Valley. It was comparatively narrow, looking straighter than it really was, from the towering Coast Range that rose in vast massive ridges, several of the peaks piercing the clouds and reaching far up into the snow line. This was indeed an impassable barrier to their further progress beyond the valley, had they wished to make the attempt; for among those wild regions, where at midsummer the snow is whirled in blinding eddies, and the storm howls through gorges and canyons, and the lost traveler gropes blindly for a secure foothold along the mountain paths—it would have been fatal for them to venture without a sure guide.

The Salinas Valley looked like a garden to them, and was indeed a promised land. There was fruit in abundance, and every prospect of meeting some of their own people. The Buenaventura, years ago, was a fabled river, and the geographies made it a huge stream, taking every course except the true one. They found it a river inferior in breadth and length to the Hudson, but vastly more interesting from its primeval character and the wild scenery along its banks.

On the eastern slope of the mountains they discerned a great variety of trees, among them the *Palo Colorado* or

Edward S. Ellis

Lambertine fir, some of them a dozen feet in diameter, although they did not attain any remarkable height. These were not the colossal pines so famous the world over. There were quite a number of beech, sycamore, oak, spruce, and maple, and other trees whose particular names they were unable to tell.

There was a noticeable change in the climate also. The air had parted with a great deal of its moisture, and although very warm, it had a dryness about it that made it more grateful and pleasant than the coolness along the coast.

When fairly in the Salinas Valley, and along the river, they found the vegetation remarkably luxuriant. Oats grew wild in many places, and the plants partook greatly of a tropical character. Grapes were very abundant, although it was too early in the season to find them ripe; yet they gathered a few berries that were very pleasant to the taste.

The first day among the hills was spent like the first one on shore—without food, although they had so gormandized themselves on the preceding evening that they were able to stand this privation much better.

On the second morning among the hills, just as they had risen and resumed their journey, Terror gave notice of something unusual in his characteristic manner—by halting and uttering a low whine. At that moment they were making their way around a huge mass of rocks, in a path that seemed to have been worn by the feet of wild animals. Tim paused, cocked his rifle and held it ready for instant use, while the boys looked around for some covert into which to retreat, if danger threatened.

While they stood in anxious suspense, an animal about the size of Terror walked leisurely into view, and catching sight of the strangers raised its head with a look of alarm, then uttered a shrill *baa-aa* after the manner of affrighted sheep, and turned to flee. But he was too valuable a prize to be let run away in this manner, and ere he could turn round, or the Newfoundland could reach him, Tim had sent a bullet through his head that tumbled him over and over as if he had been hit by a cannon-ball.

Hurrying up to him, they found they had been fortunate enough to secure a good large mountain sheep, a species of animal that run wild in California, and at certain seasons of the year are in prime condition. This was found only tolerable, but he was fully appreciated by our friends. Tim O'Rooney had managed to conceal a second knife about his person when bargaining with the Indian—one made on the liberal ideas that was displayed in the construction of his watch, and far more useful than the ornamental trifles that the boys carried.

With the help of this and the anatomical knowledge he possessed, he was not long in dressing the sheep, and everything was made ready for cooking him. The sticks were placed together, the choice steaks were suspended on cross pieces, and the leaves heaped up, only awaiting ignition.

"I declare!" exclaimed Howard, "how are we going to kindle it?"

Every face looked blank, for the thought had never entered their minds until that moment.

"Haven't yees a match about you?" he asked, turning to the boys.

Naturally enough the two searched every pocket, and having finished searched them over again, even turning them wrong

Edward S. Ellis

side out, and then turning them in and turning them wrong side out again; but all in vain, there was not a lucifer in the party.

"Too bad!" exclaimed Elwood, "we are all as hungry as we can be, and we shall have to remain so for the want of fire."

"If we wait a while we'll not need the match."

"Why not?"

"It isn't very hard to git hungry enough to ate the same without waiting for the benefit of cooking."

"I can't do that," added Elwood, with an expression of disgust.

"Nor can I," added Howard.

"I've done it, and found it tasted good," said Tim, "and so would yez—but howld on! One of yez whack me over the head!"

"For what?" they demanded in amazement.

"For being an owld fool, and be the same towken it's yourselves that is the same."

"We do not understand you," they said, in some perplexity.

"Yez are talking about fire when we has it here at hand."

They looked inquiringly around, but did not understand the allusion until he began loading the gun, when a new light broke upon them, and they smiled knowingly at each other.

Tim put in a good wadding composed of dry leaves, and placing the muzzle of his gun among the leaves that they had gathered for ignition, he discharged it. The intense flame of fire that streamed forth for an instant communicated itself to the kindlings, and this being quickly and vigorously blown by all three, almost immediately spread into a blaze, the wood gathered heat speedily, and in a few minutes the juicy steaks of the mountain sheep were steaming and ready for the voracious mouths of the four gathered around.

Edward S. Ellis

# CHAPTER XIII

## ANOTHER BARGAIN

Our friends were prudent enough to cook every available portion of the mountain sheep, and to preserve what remained for future contingencies. The climate was so warm that they could not hope to keep it more than a day or two; and, as it was, they took the wise course of placing as much of it within their stomachs as they could conveniently carry. The good-tempered red Newfoundland seemed to be growing corpulent on this species of living, protracted hunger alternating with an over supply of food.

They saw no more wild animals during the day, but just as they were entering the Salinas Valley Elwood discovered something lying in the path before them which at first he believed to be an Indian, either asleep or dead; but Terror instantly ran up, and seizing it in his teeth laid it at his feet, and discovered a beautiful Indian blanket.

"Strange!" exclaimed the boy, holding it up before him. "This shows that we are not the first persons who have traversed this section."

"I wonder that we do not see more savages."

"Isn't it beautiful?" said Elwood, turning the blanket over and examining its texture and designs. It was indeed handsome and very valuable, resembling much the famous blankets made by the Apache Indians. It was fully a half-inch in thickness, so compactly knit together as to be water-proof. Its border and the design of the figures were a miracle of skill in color and combination. Every hue of the rainbow seemed reproduced in the most pleasing combinations. The center-piece was a figure of the sun which, with the rays radiating from it, was of a most intense yellow, while around the border were pictured all the fruits that any one has ever heard as being indigenous to California.

"That must be very valuable," said Howard.

"It is so heavy it tires my arms to hold it."

"That same thing would bring yez five hundred dollars, any day, in San Francisco," added Tim O'Rooney. "It'll pay yez to carry it there."

"It is just the thing to wrap around us when we lie down to sleep."

"Yis, if ye wraps up in that yez'll wake up and find yersilves roasted to dith. Yez might as well crawl into an oven and bake yersilves and be done with it."

"We can then spread it on the ground, and protect ourselves from the moisture!" said Howard, who was beginning to appreciate the value of the article.

"I've saan them things before," added Tim O'Rooney. "The Apaches and Mohaws in New Mexico make 'em. It has tuk a couple of squaws the bist part of a year to do the same."

"But where is the owner? An Indian could not lose such a thing without knowing it. Why, it is a load to carry, and I should expect to lose my coat as soon as to part with this."

Of course there could be no explanation of the cause of the blanket being found where it was. It was plain that no Indian could have parted with it unknowingly, and its high value made it still more puzzling that it should have been left in such a place. It might be that the owner—some fragile Indian girl—had wearied with carrying it, and had thrown it down for a warrior friend of hers to pick up and take to its destination for her.

This conjecture, made by Tim O'Rooney himself, raised a serious question as to whether they had a right to carry the blanket away when there was good reason to doubt its being lost or abandoned.

"If a year's work has been lavished upon it," said Elwood, "it cannot be possible that it has no owner."

"I think Tim is right; he or she expects to return or send and get it."

"But it is singular that if such is the case it should be left here, when it could have been easily hid in these bushes."

"That only proves that there are no people about—no white ones at least. If the owner had any fear of this place being visited by *Christians*, he would have taken pains to hide his property; but as he was sure there were none but savages and heathen, he was certain his blanket was safe."

Howard Lawrence, jesting though he was, spoke the truth, and deeply ashamed are we to confess it.

The question received an unexpected and unmistakable solution. While they were still conversing, they descried a gaudily dressed, rather handsome-looking squaw tripping lightly behind them. Her head was bent, and she did not discover them until the growl of the dog caused her to raise her head. She was then within a dozen yards of Howard, he being in the rear and holding the blanket in his hand. She looked at them with an alarmed expression in her strange dark eyes, and seemed to be too much frightened to think of fleeing.

Howard signified his friendship by walking quietly toward her and holding out the blanket as if inviting her to take it. She readily comprehended the meaning of his advance, and when the article was within reach she took it.

"Now make a bargain if you can," called out Elwood.

Howard produced the gold watch—a small hunting-case—and offered it to the young woman. She examined it with childish curiosity, but in a manner that showed that it was not the first time she had looked upon such an article. She held it a for moments, and then with a pleased smile passed the blanket to him, bowed gracefully, wheeled quickly, and slipped away charmingly.

"Hurra!" fairly shouted Elwood, "you are as good as Tim at making a bargain."

"She must live somewhere about here, and no doubt will tell how she got the watch, and that may set some of her friends on our track."

"Let 'em come," said Tim. "I've a gun that I larned how to shoot, and that blanket we can wrap around us, and I don't believe you could shoot a bullet through it by raison of its thickness."

Edward S. Ellis

The party resumed their journey, quite jubilant over the rifle and blanket. They still needed but one thing, or rather two things, guns for the boys. Terror was such a sharp and faithful sentinel they would have felt almost safe with these additional fire-arms. Howard and Elwood were quite confident that they could shoot with remarkable precision, although, neither had ever aimed or discharged a gun; but in this respect they were not so very different from other boys.

At noon they made a hearty meal upon a portion of what still remained of the mountain sheep, and then stretched themselves out for an hour's rest. Tim O'Rooney was plentifully supplied with tobacco, and perhaps could not have felt more comfortable or satisfied with his situation. He lolled on the grass, and wondered whether Mr. Lawrence was anxious for him to get home or not, finally reaching the conclusion that he was rather indifferent upon the subject himself. The greatest distress of Howard and Elwood was the pain that their parents would feel regarding them; but they hoped to reach home without great delay, when they would quickly turn their weeping into joy.

The two could not grow weary of admiring their beautiful blanket. It was a wonderful affair indeed, and doubtless contained within it enough material to supply a "shoddy" contractor with the basis for a thousand army blankets. The boys would have willingly given both their watches for it and considered themselves greatly the gainers. They looked upon it as their joint property.

"I do believe it is rifle-proof," said Howard. "The fine threads of which it is composed are woven so compactly that you can hardly distinguish them."

"I should be rather fearful of risking a rifle-shot from any one if that were all that protected me."

"We can easily test it. Let's hung it up and shoot a bullet at it."

"No, that would be too bad. The ball might go through, and then it would be spoiled in its looks. Now it seems really perfect—"

"I say, me boys—"

Tim's utterance was checked by the discharge of a rifle and the near whistle of the bullet. He started up and glanced around him.

"Injuns, or me name isn't Tim O'Rooney, from Tipperary, Ireland, the gem of the say!"

Edward S. Ellis

# CHAPTER XIV

## A STRANGE OCCURRENCE

On a slight eminence, about an eighth of a mile south of them, stood the solitary Indian who had fired the alarming shot, he was in open view, as though he had no fears of the results of his challenge, and appeared to be surveying the white people with an air of curiosity that they should presume to encroach upon his hunting-grounds.

"If yez manes that, there's two of us, as me brother Pat towld the judge when he called him a good-for-nothing dog."

With which exclamation Tim O'Rooney sighted his rifle at the aborigine, and taking a tedious, uncomfortable aim, pulled the trigger, and then lowered his piece and stared at his target to watch the result. The Indian stood as motionless as a statue, and finally the Irishman drew a deep sigh.

"I wonder whether the bullet has reached him yet?"

"Reached him!" laughed Howard. "I saw it clip off a piece of rock fully forty feet from him."

"Worrah, worrah! but I've ate so much dinner I can't howld the gun stiddy."

"I saw it vibrate—"

"Look out! he's going to shoot again!" called Elwood, as he and Howard dropped on their faces. "Get down, Tim, or he'll hit you. He's a better marksman than you are."

"Who cares—Heaven! save me!"

The second discharge sent the bullet within a few inches of the Irishman's face, and somewhat alarmed him.

"Load quick!" admonished Howard, "and shelter yourself, or you are a dead man."

The Irishman obeyed this, and had his gun reloaded in a few moments.

"Now let me try my hand," said Elwood; "you can never hit him."

"Be all manes, if yez wish it."

"The piece is too heavy for me to shoot off-hand and I'll rest it on my knee."

The boy took the gun, and placing the barrel on his knee, drew back the hammer, when presto! the savage whisked out of sight like magic. The noble aborigine had come to the conclusion that discretion was the better part of valor.

"Where is he?" asked the bewildered boy, rising to his feet and looking around him.

"He is gone," replied Howard.

"I admire his sense; he doesn't care about being shot just yet."

Howard laughed.

"You have a good opinion of your marksmanship, Elwood, and he seems to fear you more than Tim."

"But he didn't give me time to practice on 'im," said the latter. "If he had stood there an hour or two I'd hit him sure."

"Yes, and he would have picked you off at the next fire. He's a good marksman at any rate."

They kept their position for some time, but saw nothing more of the Indian.

"He has left," said Elwood, "and will give us a wide berth after this."

"It was rather curious that he should expose himself in that manner."

"Perfectly natural," replied Elwood. "He knew there was no danger until *I* took the gun; then he thought it best for him to clear out."

"He may turn up again when we least expect it."

"Do yees understand the maning of that?"

"Not precisely; do you?"

"He's a lover of the fair female that ye gave the watch to for the blanket, and he had been watchin' us till he sane me, and then he got so jailous of me that he has tried to put me out of the way."

The boys laughed at this explanation, which Tim gave with

every appearance of earnestness, and were rather doubtful about believing it.

There was some fear expressed that this Indian might send them a bullet from some covert, when he could make his aim sure and shelter himself from all danger of a return fire; although as regards that the specimen he had been given of the skill of the whites should have convinced him that there was no need of his being particularly alarmed on this point.

Our friends were sufficiently rested, and the associations of the place were such that they resumed their journey at once toward the Salinas river. They had gone but a short distance when Howard exclaimed:

"Halloo! yonder goes that Indian!"

He pointed in the direction of the river fully a mile away, and looking there they saw very near the center of the stream a small Indian canoe, propelled by a single occupant. The distance was so great that they could decide nothing regarding his dress and appearance, and for a time it was doubtful whether there were one or two in the boat. They were sure, however, that it was the same personage that had so startled them, and that he was returning to his home.

"That looks as though he did not belong to these parts," said Elwood, "and seems to throw doubt on his being the young squaw's lover."

"And it's a qua'r lover the same would be if he wouldn't go five hundred miles for the smile of his beloved. Begorrah! but it was meself that used to walk five miles and back agin ivery Sunday night in Tipperary to see Bridget Ann Mulloney, and then lost her after all when I'd spent almost half a pound on her."

"There's another thing I'd like to buy, beside our rifles," said Elwood.

"What is that?"

"A canoe. See how smoothly the savage floats down the river. The current is quite rapid, and it would take very little labor for us to make much better headway than we now do.'"

"But we do not know how to paddle one of those frail concerns."

"We could learn soon enough."

"We may find one of them along the shore, as there seem to be plenty of Indians hereabouts, and I suppose every one of them is the proprietor of one of these establishments."

"It isn't likely if yees finds one ye'll find the owner," said Tim, "and I s'pose your conscience wouldn't let you take it unless you made a fair bargain with the owner."

"I don't know," laughed Howard, "but what under the circumstances we could persuade ourselves to take it."

In the course of a few hours they found themselves in the vicinity of the Salinas River, and turned to the left so as to follow its windings as nearly as possible to the mouth, where they hoped to secure safer and speedier transportation to their homes.

At night when they encamped the soft murmur of the river was in their ears, and the cool, dry wind fanned them quietly as they sat down near a cluster of thick cottonwood to smoke their pipe, chat and prepare for the night's rest. They made a good meal from their mountain sheep, and gorging Terror, threw the rest away as they deemed it hardly fit for further use.

It was quite late when they camped. Tim would have nothing to do with the blanket, so the boys spread it upon the earth, lay down upon it, and then drew the borders over them.

Wearied out they soon fell asleep, depending, under the kindness of heaven, upon the watchfulness of the faithful Newfoundland that had never yet proved unfaithful to his trust.

In the middle of the night Elwood awoke from a feeling of uncomfortable warmth, and threw the blanket off and slept thus until morning. He was the first to awake, just as light was dawning, and was on the point of rising when he started and became suddenly transfixed with horror at a sight directly before his eyes!

# CHAPTER XV

# THE CROTALUS

There are several species of rattlesnakes found in California, among which are the black, spotted and striped. Some of them grow to an enormous size and are anything but pleasant strangers to encounter, especially when you come upon them suddenly and find them coiled. It is a peculiarity of these specimens of the *Crotalus* of America that they strike only from the coil, are easily killed, and generally, although *not always*, do they rattle before they dart forward their poisonous fangs.

We can conceive of nothing upon the face of this beautiful earth more shudderingly repulsive than a rattlesnake. The arrowy head, and shiny, flabby body, with its glistening scales and variegated color, its tapering tail, with that dreadful arrangement by which it imitates so closely the *whirr* of the locust, the bead-like eyes, with no lids and a fleshy film dropping over them—all these make up the most terrible reptile found on the American continent.

And then imagine one of these creatures *coiled*! The thick, heavy body with the tail projecting upward from the center, the head drawn back, and the red, cavernous mouth open, with the curved, hollow teeth and the sacs at their roots filled nigh to bursting with this concentrated essence of the vilest of all poison—imagine this, we say—but don't do it either! If you have never seen a rattlesnake, don't go near one, unless you have a chance to kill it, even if his fangs have been extracted. The heel shall bruise the serpent, and that is the best use to which they can be put.

But as Howard Lawrence opened his eyes, in the dull light of this summer morning, he saw coiled within five feet of him a striped rattlesnake, its intensely black eyes fairly scintillating light, and its rattle gently waving but making no noise.

In a single second his true peril flashed upon him. If he moved the reptile would strike. He might throw himself suddenly backward, but in that case if he escaped, the malignant fangs would be buried in the sleeping Elwood ere he could open his eyes and understand the danger that threatened him. And he was afraid, too, to speak to him and Tim in the hope of awaking them. There would be blundering upon their part, and blundering meant but one thing—death.

Howard looked straight at the serpent's eyes and became conscious of a strange sensation passing through him. The small, black orbs seemed to advance, shrink and float away through the air, enchaining his own vision until the will, which had so vehemently repelled the danger grew indifferent, and the thought of peril merged into a vague, dreamy semi-consciousness, which, while it took knowledge of the terrible reptile, coiled and ready to strike, yet failed to impress the mind with the energy to withdraw from its terrible power. His blood slowly chilled, as if vein by vein it froze throughout his person, until from head to foot the vital current was congealed. At times he strove to move, or more properly sought, in the mysterious make-up of our composition, to rouse the will from its torpor, but with the same result as follows the effort of the sufferer to use his paralyzed limb. The will seemed to make a feeble twitch or two and then subside, unable to break the fatal spell spreading over his mind and faculties. The eyes of the reptile glared upon his own, their bead-like blackness taking the form of a point of fire waving, floating, gyrating and circling in the air, doubling in and out in rings of the rainbow's hues, melting away into the distance, then drifting forward until mingled with his own, up and down in the same bewildering maze of color and design that visits the patient when lost in the delirium of fever. And all the time it was as if the rattlesnake was conscious of the dreadful power he held over his victim. Its arrowy head and long neck were started silently toward him, as if threatening instant destruction; and then, like the cat toying with her victim, it was withdrawn again, and the spell deepened and increased. A strange whirl passed through the mind of the boy. By a violent attempt to call in his wandering thoughts he gathered an idea of the mortal danger impending over him, but he could not centralize his mental powers.

The bewildering sensations were somewhat similar to that of a man whose brain has received a violent concussion—the mysterious chambers and channels through which thought forced its way were choked up and the subtle impetus recoiled, powerless to perform its function. He felt the necessity of clear, vigorous thought, but his dull brain would not work—the cold incubus upon it chilled it through and through; and all the time the malignantly beautiful reptile was partly coiling and uncoiling, the articulated ring giving a faint rattle, as if caused by the slight vibration of its body. After a while the serpent lay still, but never once was its eye removed from its victim. It was growing tired of dallying with its prey and was making ready to strike. The coil became close and compact, the rattle rising from the center, and the eye assumed a clear, metallic sharpness that appeared to throw forward its fateful rays into his own. He saw that the sport was done and the snake was ready to strike; he strove to move, but could not; he essayed to speak, but the words choked him unuttered. He saw the reptile calling in its strength and—

*"Quick, Howard, draw the blanket over you! He can't strike through that!"*

The practical, energetic words of Elwood Brandon, whom he had imagined asleep at his side, broke the dreadful spell that had enchained Howard. He felt the mist pass from his eyes, his mind threw off the incubus which had borne it down, and he was himself again, with clear mental powers.

His right hand lay upon the thick blanket, and sensible of his extreme peril, he quickly closed it, grasping the edge firmly, and then threw himself over upon his face and against his cousin, but covering both their bodies at the same instant with the heavy, closely-knit cloth.

At the very moment of doing so the angry locust-like ring of the reptile and a sharp thrust against the blanket as if struck by a small stick announced that it has given its blow.

Howard and Elwood both shouted to Tim to come to their assistance; but ere he could respond a rush was heard, followed by a fierce growl, and they understood at once that Terror had appeared upon the scene.

They let him rage for a few moments and then, Tim having informed them that the snake was "kilt entirely," they cautiously crept forth. As they looked furtively around they saw at once that the Newfoundland had done his work well. The reptile was torn into shreds and strewn over an area of several yards. Its fangs had entered the blanket where, while

Edward S. Ellis

they did not pierce through they stuck irrevocably, holding the reptile a prisoner to the fury of the dog.

Thankful indeed were the boys for their providential escape from this dreaded creature. Elwood had been awakened by its slight rattling, when, suspecting the danger that was closing around his cousin, he uttered the warning words which we have given and which proved the means of robbing the blow of the reptile of its danger.

The fangs were carefully extracted from the blanket, and Howard declared his intention of preserving them as a curiosity; but within a half-hour after leaving the camp they were lost, and he did not judge it worth while to search for them.

# CHAPTER XVI

## THE CAMP-FIRE

As our three friends on that bright summer morning stood on the slope of the mountains and gazed down into the beautiful Salinas Valley before them, Elwood Brandon suddenly pointed a little to the north and said:

"See! there are others beside us!"

About a mile distant, and not far from the river, they saw a thin, black column of smoke rising among the trees, of so dark and palpable a character that it could be distinguished at once.

"Another party of Indians," replied Howard. "We seem to be getting into their neighborhood."

"I only wish they were a party of white hunters or miners, for I long to see a friendly face."

"What good could it do us? They wouldn't accompany us home, or take any trouble to see that we were protected."

"Perhaps not, but I tell you, Howard, this begins to look dangerous when we see nothing but enemies. There are but

Edward S. Ellis

three of us, and one gun only between us. I believe a single Indian could destroy us all if he chose to do so."

"Except in one contingency."

"What is that?"

"That you should aim the gun. He would then flee at once."

Elwood laughed and added:

"But we have no breakfast, and we may as well be moving."

"You're a sensible boy," added Tim O'Rooney, "be the towken that when ye spakes ye quiverally anticipates me own thoughts."

They soon reached the level of the valley, and then took a direction straight toward the spot where they had seen the camp-fire burning. The intervening space was quite thickly grown with trees and vegetation, so that they could obtain no sight of the fire itself until they were very close to it.

"We must be careful," admonished Howard. "If it is a party of Indians they may discover us before we do them."

"I don't suppose it will do for us all to walk straight up to them, for they'll be sure to see us then."

"No, one must creep up and find whether the coast is clear. Tim has seen more of California than we have, and he can do that if he wishes."

"Sinsible agin, for I was about to spake the same. Do yees tarry here while I takes a look around. Whist! now, and kaap so still that ye'll hear me brathe all the way there and back agin."

The boys took their position each behind a large tree, and looking cautiously forth they awaited the return of their friend.

When these precautions were taken they were not a hundred yards distant from the strangers. The Irishman stepped very carefully, moving on tiptoe, and not making any noise that was perceptible. This was no great attainment in woodcraft, as any person could have done the same with ordinary care, when the woods were of the character of this one. Had there been briers or brambles, or swampy ground, or that which was unusually dry, and covered with twigs, it would have been a feat far more difficult of attainment.

Just before Tim disappeared from view they saw him sink down upon his hands and knees and creep forward; but the bushes soon shut him out from view and they could only wait with all the patience possible.

At the end of about ten minutes the genial face of the Irishman appeared, and the expression upon it gave rise to pleasant anticipations.

"Who are they?" asked the two boys together, as soon as they deemed it prudent.

"Whist! now don't spake so loud. Ye'll wake 'em out."

Tim looked behind, and became satisfied that there was no fear of discovery, when he arose to his feet, and took his careless, sauntering manner.

"Well, Tim!'" said Howard inquiringly.

"What is it yez wishes?"

"We wish to know whether these strangers are white men or Indians."

"Well, ye saas, I had to crawl up to 'em mighty careful, for if you step upon a stick no bigger than a tooth-pick, yees are sortin to wake up a slaapin' copper-skin—"

"So they were Indians, then," interrupted Elwood somewhat impatiently.

"Do yes be aisy now, and not be interruptin' of me, and yer observations and questions which ain't naaded in this case. Me owld grandfather used to till a great many stories to us spalpaans about the part he took with young Emmett—when owld Ireland stood up against England. He used to tell us his stories—did the same—and just so sure as one of us axed him a question, he'd go back to the beginning and till the whole story over again. He'd begin airly in the evening, and kaap it going till tin or eleven o'clock. I belave the old gintleman rather liked to have us be interruptin' him, for he laid bates for us wee ones, and ye see by that manes one story sometimes kept him going for a waak. Heaven bliss the owld gintleman—he had a habit of stopping in the middle of an exciting part and lighting his dudheen, and then when he'd begin again, he'd skip over a part on purpose to make us ax him a question—"

"Well, Tim, we will talk about your grandfather some other day," said Howard, who, as naturally may be supposed, was impatient for him to come to the point.

"Yis, I was just through with him, but yees should never be overmuch in haste. Me blessed mother always told me that it was the same as being too slow, and if anybody could spake of the same, could me mother do it. I was about to obsarve when yees interrupted me, that a man must be mighty careful in going up to a camp-fire, for these Indians slaap so quietly that the overturning of a leaf is sure to wake 'em, and you saa by this, if we'd all three gone up, as we war thinkin' about, they'd heard us long before we could have got sight of 'em, and our tramping in Californy would be done with—"

"So they were Indians were they?" asked Elwood again, partly amused and partly vexed at Tim's persistent dallying with their curiosity.

"Who said the same?"

"You implied it. Were they red or white men? Answer us—yes or no!"

"And that is just the pint I's raching for, as me frind, Michael O'Shanghangly, said when he took a half-quart of whisky. Yez understands that I wanted to make sure just who the same might be, and what was their number. 'Spose, now, I should have come back and said there war but three of the same, and there should be a half-dozen, or I should say they was white gintlemen like ourselves, and they should turn out to be of a darker hue. Ye saas that it wouldn't do."

The boys had become so uneasy by this time that they were walking back and forth, and talking to each other in low tones.

"I will go forward and see for myself," said Elwood. "I don't care about waiting an hour or two for him to answer my question."

"He will soon answer us; he is only indulging in a little pleasantry."

"Rather a bad time for jesting."

"I think we can be sure of one thing," added Howard a moment later.

"What is that?"

"That we are not in much danger. If we were he wouldn't wait so long to tell us."

"I don't know about that; it would be in keeping with his foolishness. I tell you, Howard, I will ask him once more, and if he doesn't answer me at once, I shall go forward and learn for myself."

"Well, do so."

"Tim, are those Indians or white men?"

"That's it, is it? Why didn't yez ax me before? They're a party of white men, be the same!"

# CHAPTER XVII

## THE MINERS

"I wished to give yez a pleasant surprise, as the doctor said when he told the man that his wife was dead," remarked Tim, in explanation of his conduct. "Had there really been any of the red gintlemen around I'd have told you soon enough."

Our young friends were too well pleased at the intelligence to feel other than good natured, and they gladly forgave Tim for his trespass upon their patience. Without waiting further they walked hastily forward, and a moment later stood by the camp-fire.

Three men, apparently, had just aroused themselves from slumber, and were now stirring around making preparations for their breakfast. They were shaggy, unshorn, grimy-looking fellows, who had "run wild" for several years, but who had not necessarily lost their humanity, even though they had in a great degree lost its outward semblance. In the center, a large bundle of sticks were burning quite briskly, and one of the men was turning and watching some meat that was cooking over it. The others had evidently just returned from the river, for their red temples and foreheads still glistened with moisture which sparkled like dew on their patriarchal beards.

Edward S. Ellis

They were rough, hardy-looking fellows, but Elwood felt little apprehension as he stepped forward and said:

"Good morning, gentlemen!"

He who was cook turned his head, but a hot drop of moisture from the steaming meat at that moment flew in his eye, and clapping his finger to it, he muttered something, and forthwith and instantly gave his exclusive attention to his culinary duties.

The second man was rubbing his face with a piece of coarse cloth, and he suddenly paused with his black eyes glaring over the top, his face resembling the head of some huge animal clambering over the edge of a rock, and who, having just gained a foothold, is looking hurriedly around for his prey.

The third was combing his hair, and just at this moment it was moistened and sticking straight over his forehead like the horn of an animal. He would run the comb through with his right hand and then smooth the hair with his left. He stopped with both arms crooked over his head, and wheeled around like an automaton, and stared at the boy a moment, and then said:

"Well, there! Why didn't you ring the door-bell? I say, youngster, come forward and give us a grip of your hand. Halloo! you've got your brother with you!"

"Not my brother, but my cousin, Howard Lawrence."

The two boys shook hands with the three, and the grip that they received from the horny palms made them wince with pain.

"But where'd you come from? We don't see a couple of youngsters dressed up in your style promenading 'round in these parts every day. Where'd you come from?"

"The steamer on which we took passage the other day from Panama, was burned off the coast, and we got ashore on a raft."

"Be you the only ones?"

"No; there were quite a number that escaped."

"Where be they?"

"They were carried away by a vessel while we had wandered inland."

"And you two—halloo! here's your grandfather!"

"No; that is Tim O'Rooney, a good friend of ours."

"Your humble sarvint!" saluted the Irishman, removing his hat, making a profound bow and scraping a large foot upon the ground.

"Well, there! We're glad to see you. What's all your names?"

They were given several times, and then carefully spelled at the request of the large-whiskered man, who desired that no mistake might be made.

"You may call me Ned Trimble, and that ugly-looking fellow 'tending to the fire is George Wakeman, and that horrid-looking chap scrubbing off his dirty face, is Alfred Wilkins. Neither of them know much, and I brought them along to black my boots and dress my hair."

It looked as though Ned was a sort of a wag, for his companions smiled as if they were used to that thing. He continued:

"We're a party of hunters that have been in Californy for the last five years, and I rather guess I've prospected through every part of it."

"You must be rich by this time."

"Rich!" laughed Ned Trimble. "Well there, we're everything but rich. Somehow or other we hain't had the luck. We sold a claim up in the diggings for five hundred dollars, and the next week the party sold it for fifteen thousand. That's the way it has always gone with us; but we are going to be rich yet—ain't we, boys."

"Yes, if we only live long enough," replied Wakeman.

"I told you that chap hadn't much sense," remarked Ned, addressing his three visitors. "He doesn't know enough to answer a question as he oughter. I've been trying to teach him something, but I shall have to give it up as a bad job. Been to breakfast?"

"No—not yet."

"Thought you hadn't. Cook, put up another slice, douse it in butter, salt and pepper, and serve it up as you used to do when I employed you at the Astor. Gentlemen, how do you like it, rare or well done?"

All made answer that they were not particular, and Ned replied thereunto as follows:

"Sensible fellows! If you don't care what you get, you won't have to care much for what you don't get. What will you select as a dessert? Plum, rice, bread, or cherry pudding? Apple, mince, cranberry, plum, peach, or lemon pie? Cup-custard, tapioca, watermelon, citron, or sherry, maderia, or port. Order which ever you choose, gentlemen, it don't make any difference to us. We can give you one just as well as the other."

"I suppose you can," laughed Howard; "so we'll not take the trouble to order any."

"All right; as you please, gentlemen. We haven't any turkey or oysters left so you will have to put up with a little antelope that we shot yesterday afternoon. Fine condition for this time of year, and the best kind of flesh to starve to death on."

"We haven't had a taste of it yet; but we devoured a goodly piece of a mountain sheep."

"Just so. I was going to speak of a mountain sheep, if my servants hadn't interrupted me so often with inquiries as to how they should make the wine sauce. Ah! I see our meal is ready; we will therefore repair to the banquet hall."

The six took their seats upon the leaves, and ate the meal in the usual primitive manner, verifying the adage, "hunger is the best sauce."

Ned Trimble enlivened the meal in his usual loquacious manner; and after a great many words and circumlocution, the fact was discovered that he and his friends had spent the last five years in California, not having visited a civilized post within two years.

Disgusted with their ill success in the Sacramento Valley, they had pulled up stakes and started off to hunt new fields for

Edward S. Ellis

themselves. They were very cheerful and hopeful, and according to their accounts had encountered every imaginable danger of the California wilds.

Elwood inquired whether they had met any grizzly bears.

"Grizzly bears!" repeated Ned, stopping just as he was about to insert a huge piece of meat in his mouth. "Grizzly bears? Well, there! *We've lived among 'em!*"

"Is it possible?"

"Yes; I tracked a big grizzly in the Sierra Nevada for two days and then I stopped."

"What made you stop?"

*"I concluded the bear tracks were getting a little too fresh!"*

# CHAPTER XVIII

## A WANT SUPPLIED

One thing attracted the notice and pleased our friends, and gave them a hope of being able to supply a want they had felt every moment since landing upon the California coast. Each of the miners had two rifles, and were abundantly supplied with ammunition and mining tools. The wonder was how they could carry so heavy a load for such a distance. It could not be understood until Ned Trimble stated that they had two good, tough mules pasturing in a secluded place about a half-mile distant.

"That 'ere Injin blanket you're carryin' is rather pretty!" remarked Ned as he rubbed his greasy fingers through his hair.

"Yes, we got it of an Indian girl, and take great pride in it."

"You did, eh? What did you give her for it?"

"A gold watch."

"Ah! Well, if the watch was a first-rate one maybe she got her pay; but what did she want with a watch? That's just the way with all women. They'll give ten times the value for some little gewgaw to wear about 'em. I was engaged to a fine-looking girl in North Carolina, but I seen she was getting so extravagant that I couldn't understand it, so I left before it was too late."

"A very wise plan."

"Yes, she was very extravagant."

"In what respect?" asked Elwood, who was quite amused at their newly-found friend.

"Well, you see, she would persist in wearing shoes on Sunday instead of going barefoot like the rest of the young ladies. I warned her two or three times, but I catched her at church one day with them on, and so I went over to the house that night and told her I couldn't trust her any longer, and we exchanged presents and parted."

"Exchanged presents?" laughed Wakeman. "What sort of presents were they?"

"I wish no trifling insinuations, sir," replied Ned, with a grandiloquent air. "She returned to me a tooth brush that I had presented her some months before, and I gave back to her a tin button that she had bought of a traveling peddler, and that I had been wearing on Sundays for my breastpin. 'Tis not the intrinsic worth you know, but the associations connected with such things that makes 'em dear. But it is a painful subject, gentlemen, and let us, therefore, dismiss it."

Howard and Lawrence thought it best to introduce the matter upon which they had been so long meditating.

"I notice that each of you have two guns apiece. Did you leave San Francisco with that supply?"

"No; we've got 'em of the redskins we've run agin on the way."

"Would you be willing to sell us a couple? You observe we have but one between us, and it makes it rather dangerous, as none of us are very skillful in the use of the rifle."

"You needn't take the trouble to tell us that," replied Ned, with a quizzical look. "I'd like to accommodate you, but we had begun to think that we needed three or four guns apiece; for, you see, we intend to stay in these parts some time, and we are sure to have trouble with the redskins."

"If you really wish them," remarked Elwood, "of course we cannot ask you to part with them."

"What'll you give?" abruptly asked Ned.

"What will you take?"

"I couldn't sell you both of mine, as I wouldn't have one; but, Wakeman, if I part with one of mine will you do the same?"

"Yes; for I know they'll need the arms before they get back to San Francisco."

"Then the question is, what will you ask us for the two guns?"

"Can you give us a hundred dollars?"

"Apiece?"

"No, no, no; for both of 'em."

"Yes; we will gladly do that."

Edward S. Ellis

Now came the crisis. The party had not a dozen dollars among them. Howard and Elwood had left their money in the berth of the steamer, and of course it was irrevocably gone. But Elwood's watch remained, and that at the least calculation was worth one hundred and fifty; but whether the miners would accept it at a fair valuation for their pieces, was in their minds very doubtful.

"We have no money," said Howard, "but my cousin has a watch that is worth more than that sum, which he will give you for the two guns."

"Let's see it."

It was produced and passed around the company. Ned opened and shut it, and shook it and placed it to his ear.

"It ain't running," he suddenly said.

"No; the salt water has stopped it, but I do not think it is really injured. A little cleaning will speedily set it going."

Ned passed the time-piece back again.

"Don't want it; it won't do us no good."

"But you are hunting for gold, and there is enough in it to make it worth your while to take it."

"We expect to find all the gold we can carry back with us without loading our mules down with gold watches."

Elwood replaced the watch in his pocket, disheartened at the failure of his offer.

"We have no money; if you will call at my father's the next

time you go to San Francisco, he will gladly give you your price."

"Don't know as we shall go to San Francisco for the next five years; shan't go any way until we are loaded down with gold, and then we won't care about calling on your father—more likely he'll want to call on us."

An idea struck Howard.

"You are pleased with our blanket. Will you exchange your guns for that?"

Ned shook his head.

"Got all the blankets we want; don't want it; keep it yourself."

"Will you not give us one gun for both the blanket and watch?"

The miner now laughed, and shook his head again.

"Don't want either; can't do it."

The boys now despaired.

"Well, we may as well give up. We can't get any guns of you."

"What is the reason you can't?"

"You seem unwilling to trade, and we can not buy them."

"Of course you can't; but—"

And thereupon the miner rose to his feet and handed one gun to Elwood and the other to Howard.

"What does this mean?" asked the latter, not comprehending him.

"You don't suppose we would be *mean* enough to *sell* you anything you needed so bad, do you? No; take them both, and here's a lot of lead, gun-caps and ammunition."

"But—"

"No *buts* about it. Take 'em, you're welcome, for you need 'em. I was only joking with you."

# CHAPTER XIX

## THE CANOE

Ned Trimble would not hear the repeated thanks of our friends, but waved them an impressive and magnificent farewell as they took their departure. They were not yet beyond sight of each other when they heard him calling to them in excited tones, and the next moment he came running after them.

"I think you said you was going to undertake to foller the river down the valley, didn't you?"

They made answer that such was their intention, whereupon he hastened to add:

"About a mile down, under some bushes that stick out by a big rock, on the same side that you're traveling, is a little Injin canoe that is just the thing you want. You're welcome to it."

"But how shall we thank you?"

"I don't know; again, my noble friends, I bid thee farewell, and if forever, still forever, fare thee well."

Edward S. Ellis

The eccentric miner lifted his hat, bowed very low, and sauntered back to his friends with the air of a monarch who had just indulged in some gracious act of condescension, while our friends, delighted beyond measure, hurried forward on their journey.

They were now amply provided—each having a gun and plenty of ammunition, and their faithful dog. They began to look upon themselves as on a holiday excursion. The only thing was, that there was rather too strong a tinge of danger about it. If they were but a hundred or two miles nearer home, and their parents had no anxiety regarding them, it would be more pleasant. But then, they could easily understand how much worse it easily could be, and they were heartfelt at the good fortune which had followed them thus far on their strange entry into California. The most that they could ask was that it might continue.

Elwood and Howard were anxious to test their marksmanship, but prudence forbade it, as the chances were that they would need all their ammunition, and the report of their guns might draw inconvenient attention to themselves.

They were walking cheerily along when a singular object caught their eyes. At first sight it resembled an Indian hut; but it was much too small to be inhabited by a human being, and therefore must have been the handiwork of some animal.

"Shall we batter it down?" asked Elwood.

"No; we do not know what is in it, and there is no use of wantonly destroying the home of any dumb creature."

"It reminds me of me birthplace in ould Ireland," said Tim, with a sigh.

But Terror was not so considerate as his masters; for bursting forward he placed his snout at the lower orifice, snuffed furiously, and then clawed so savagely that the greater part of the singular fabric came tumbling to the ground. It was made of brush and twigs, and like everything constructed by instinct, was put together with great skill. Terror could not be restrained until he had inflicted great injury.

"Look! what are they?" exclaimed Howard in astonishment. "What strange-looking creatures!"

"Snapping tortles!" replied Tim, staring with an expression of the greatest astonishment at the objects.

Three animals, about the size of a musk-rat, with webbed feet, and the color of mice, came scrambling forth and scampered away for the shelter of the rocks.

Terror by this time had been brought under restraint, and was prevented from crushing them to death as they ran.

Great speculation was caused by their appearance, as none of our friends had seen anything like them, nor had they ever heard or read of such. They were, in fact, a species of mountain rat living in the vicinity of mountains and constructing their singular-looking huts with remarkable skill, often building them to a height of six feet. Their fur is very fine, and the hunters and trappers frequently take the animals for their coats, although their diminutive size, when compared with the beaver, otter, and other fur-bearing animals, prevents their being much in demand.

The hunters, as perhaps it is proper to term them, were too anxious to discover the canoe to pause long at any curiosity unless it was something extraordinary. They carefully noted the distance they journeyed, and when they judged they had gone about a mile, stepped into the edge of the river and looked about them. But they saw nothing answering to Ned Trimble's description of the hiding-place of the boat.

"Perhaps he was jesting," remarked Elwood.

"No; I think he is too kind-hearted for that. He may have been mistaken as to whether it is precisely a mile or not."

"Whist! but it strikes me that the bushes are rather thick just ayonst you."

Tim pointed to a spot a hundred rods away which had failed to arrest their attention. There was nothing unusual, except mayhap that the overhanging shrubbery was rather denser than usual; but it held out hope, and the party hurried pell-mell to the spot.

There, sure enough, they descried the rock, and lifting the bushes, caught sight of the small, delicate canoe concealed beneath. Elwood was in the advance, and quickly pulled it forth with the wildest expressions of delight.

"Isn't it splendid!" he fairly shouted. "And here is a long paddle. Our work is now done."

"Do yees jist stand up in the same," said Tim, "and see what a beautiful rest it gives to the faat."

The impulsive boy caught up the paddle, and rose to his feet; but it was like unto him who first puts on skates. It flashed from beneath him, and he was precipitated headlong into the water. The others, as a matter of course, laughed.

"That was done on purpose," said Elwood as he clambered to his feet again.

"I wished to give yees a little insthruction, and that was me first lesson."

"Well, I learned considerable at any rate."

The canoe was caught, and the three carefully entered and seated themselves. It was made of bark, bound together with cord and gum, and would have held double their weight, being very light and buoyant.

A vast amount of sport was afforded the party in learning to navigate the frail vessel. Tim had had some experience in the matter, and could propel it quite dexterously; but the boys were much at fault: they expended far more strength than there was any need for, and soon exhausted themselves so thoroughly that they were obliged to relinquish the sole management of the boat into the hands of Tim O'Rooney.

"There's a bootiful current here," said he, "and we can have the illegant pleasure of moving along without working ourselves, as me frind, Michael McGubbens, said when they carried him off to Botany Bay."

The Irishman first dipped his paddle upon the one side and then upon the other, and imparted quite a velocity to the canoe. The boys were so pleased with the easy, gliding motion that they failed to notice the shores they were passing between. When finally Tim lay down his paddle and rested they were charmed.

All were tired enough to make them enjoy this relaxation and the sensation of floating so idly forward. The sky was clear and almost free of clouds, the dry air was not uncomfortably warm, and an occasional breeze that came floating apparently from the snowy peaks of the Coast Range imparted delicious coolness. On the left stretched the high hills intervening between them and the Pacific, and on the right rose the vast Coast Mountains, forming in its extensive line some of the finest scenery on the North American Continent.

By-and-by, as they rounded a bend in the river, a small island appeared near the center of the channel.

"There we will rest," said Howard.

A half-hour later the canoe lightly touched the shore, and springing out they pulled it up on the land after them. They had scarcely done so when a groan very near them startled them all.

"Whisht!" whispered Tim; "there's somebody else beside us on this island."

# CHAPTER XX

## SHASTA, THE PAH UTAH

All three paused and listened. For a moment all was still; and then the suppressed groan of distress was heard, as though the sufferer were seeking to keep back the outcry that was forced from him.

"There it is!" whispered Howard, pointing to a clump of bushes near the edge of the river.

"It strikes me we had better leave!" replied Elwood, looking forward to the canoe as if fearful that that would be taken from them and all escape be thus cut off.

"Do you sind the dog forward and let him smell out the difficulty," suggested Tim O'Rooney.

Terror stood there between the boys, his head raised and his whole appearance indicating that he had scented something unusual, but was awaiting orders before advancing upon it. The Newfoundland looked up as if asking for directions. Elwood simply pointed toward the brush and the dog galloped to it. Instead of entering, he stopped by it and gave a low growl of discovery.

Edward S. Ellis

"What is it, Terror?" asked Howard.

The brute whined and ran to his masters and then back to the bushes.

"It maybe a trap to catch us," said Elwood. "I prefer very much taking to the canoe and getting away from the island."

"But it may be some one suffering and needing help. He may perish if we leave him here."

"Yez spakes the truth," said Tim. "The blessed Father would never forgive us if we should desart one of his creatures when he needed hilp."

Tim now advanced straight to the bushes, paused, and then parted them and looked in. He was heard to mutter something to himself; then he came back.

"It's an Injin, a-layin' on the ground, a-groanin' and a-rollin' over. I guess the poor fellow has got his last sickness, and we can't help him any."

All feelings were at once merged into that of pity. The three advanced and parted the bushes. There, sure enough, lay an Indian apparently nigh unto death. He turned his black eyes up to the white people in a manner that would have melted the heart of a Nero. He lay doubled up on his blanket, with his gun a short distance from him. He belonged to the Pah Utah tribe, although their hunting-grounds are further to the southwest. This fact, as a matter of course, was unknown to our friends.

The first impression was that he had been badly wounded, but a second glance showed that he was deadly sick.

Elwood Brandon had placed his hand upon the dusky forehead, and the heat and throbbing temples told him at once that he was possessed with a burning fever.

The poor Indian muttered something unintelligible, but which bore some resemblance to the word "Shasta," and he made a motion toward his mouth and then threw his head back and imitated the act of drinking.

"He must be suffering with thirst," said Howard. "How shall we manage to give him water?"

"God save the poor fellow! I will soon fix that!" exclaimed the kind-hearted Tim, rising to his feet and hurrying to the river's edge. Here he speedily constructed quite a capacious cup of leaves, and carefully filling it with cool water he as carefully carried it back to where he lay.

"Now, me good felly, just tip up his noddle and we'll make him faal aisy."

Elwood carefully raised his head, and the trembling sufferer eagerly reached forward for the cooling fluid. It was placed to his parched lips and swallowed hastily, when he immediately motioned for more.

"Will it do to give it?" asked Howard. "Will it not injure him?"

"Niver a bit," replied Tim, hurrying away for another supply.

In a moment it was brought and swallowed with the same avidity. He then lay his head back upon the blanket of the boys, which had been folded into a pillow by Howard. His great black eyes looked the thanks which his tongue was unable to express.

Edward S. Ellis

"Now he will slaap," said Tim. "Lave him alone."

He was relinquished to slumber while our friends retired a short distance to consult.

"How providential that we landed here," said Howard. "He was too feeble to help himself, and might have died in great distress."

"Yes, I am glad that we found him, for if he does die we may be the means of robbing his last moments of great suffering."

"Boys," said Tim, hitching up his pantaloons and scratching his head, "me mind is made up to one thing."

The boys looked inquiringly at him.

"I stays here till that poor copper-skin gets well or dies."

This decision pleased his companions, who declared their resolve of doing all they could for the sufferer.

"How much more pleasant than shooting at him," said Elwood. "I never felt better in my life than when I found I was able to do something for this Indian."

What a happiness it is indeed to minister to the wants of the suffering and distressed! What purer joy than to wipe away the damp from the brow of the dying and to speak words of consolation in their ears? That last agony must come to us all sooner or later, and oh how deeply we shall then appreciate the kindness of the friend who stands beside us, ministering to our wants and doing all possible to cheer and soothe our suffering! True, we must go alone through the Dark Valley, but others may lead us down to the border, and their cheering words may yet linger with us as the day closes and we step into that awful gloom through which we must pass before we can enter into the eternal day beyond. Though we know that He stands waiting to take our hand in His and lead us through the solemn darkness, yet the soul, hovering in its flight, longs for the companionship of the dear ones, until the final adieu must come! Oh, loving Father, whose sympathizing arms reach out to enfold us all, grant that such may be mine and the lot of all my friends.

Upon looking at the Indian an hour later, he was seen to be sleeping as calmly as an infant, while his face was covered with a mild, healthful moisture.

"He will git well!" said Tim. "Did I not stand by the bedside of my poor mother and give her the cowld water that brought her back to life agin?"

"The crisis of the fever has passed, or is passing," said Howard. "He must have an iron constitution, like all his people, and he will rally, I have no doubt."

"Yes," added Elwood, with much feeling, "there is one thing certain; *all* are not our enemies; we have made one friend at least."

"True, an Indian never forgets an injury nor a kindness, and his friendship may be of benefit to us before we reach home."

"I b'laves you, boys; that Injin will remember us as long as he lives, and will sarve us a good turn if the chances for the same be iver given him."

"But see, he has awaked!"

# CHAPTER XXI

## A HUNT FOR FOOD

The Indian was awake and making signs to his friends. For some time they were at a loss to understand their meaning, but Howard noticed that he had a leaf in his hand which he offered to them. When the boy took it his face showed that he was pleased, but continued his signs as before.

Suddenly Elwood's eyes sparkled.

"He wants us to bring him some of those leaves. Let me have it; they must be on the island."

He hastened away and was not long in finding a bush that bore precisely the same species, and gathering quite a lot he returned to the Indian and offered them to him. But he did not seem satisfied. He looked at the leaves, nodded his head, and then taking them by the slight twigs to which they were fastened, he made as if to pull them up again.

"Ah! I know what he means!" said Howard. "It is not the leaf but the root that he wishes."

"I can soon get that."

Elwood verified his words, and scarce ten minutes elapsed ere he returned with several goodly-sized roots, which were washed and cleaned. The look of the Indian showed that he had now got what he wanted, and he began gnawing the bark and chewing it.

"He's a docthering himself now!" said Tim, "as the patient said when he gave the docther his own medicine and pisened him to death by raisin of the same. He will get along."

They watched the sufferer for a few moments. Gathering his mouth nearly full of the bark, he continued chewing and swallowing for some time longer, when he finally shut his eyes and again slept.

Picking up a piece of the root which he had gathered Elwood tasted of it. He found it so bitter that he instantly spat it out.

"It must have some medicinal quality," remarked Howard, "or he would not use it. I believe the Indians doctor entirely with herbs, and I have no doubt that he will soon be well."

"Do yez mind that if it isn't noon it is close to the same? And be the tame towken we are all slightly hungry."

Now arose a query. The island was so small that it contained no game of any kind, and so was unavailable to supply their wants. The river abounded in fish, but there was no means of catching them; and finally, after some discussion, it was agreed that Tim should cross over to the mainland and shoot something.

"Do yez kaap your eyes about yez till I'z back again, for some of the coppery gintlemen may take a notion to pay yez a visit."

Edward S. Ellis

The boys felt a little uneasiness as they saw their companion enter the canoe and paddle toward the eastern shore—the shore which as yet had been unvisited by them. They watched until he landed, pulled the boat up behind him into shelter, and then disappeared in the wood.

"We shall be in rather a bad situation if he never comes back," remarked Elwood.

"I don't know about that; in what better occupation can we be found than in ministering to the wants of a suffering Indian? Would not that itself protect us from injury?"

"Perhaps it might; but what would become of us any way? They wouldn't be kind enough to guide us up to San Francisco."

"They might take us so far that we could find our way."

"Hardly; I don't like to see Tim go to that shore; it looks too dangerous. I wonder why he did it?"

"He must have believed there is more game there."

"But there is enough on the other side, and he would avoid this greater danger by going there."

"I imagine that a river running through a hostile country is as dangerous upon one side as upon the other, and there is little choice, Howard, in the matter."

"But I know *you* feel unpleasant in being thus left alone."

"I know I shall be glad to see Tim come back again, for there is always great danger in such a small party separating."

"Halloo! there goes his gun or somebody else's."

The sharp crack of the rifle came from the shore, and Elwood was sure he saw the faint smoke of the discharge ascend from some thick bushes near the edge of the wood. But he was no doubt mistaken, for as they scrutinized the spot they detected nothing of him who had fired the gun.

"I suppose it was Tim firing at some game. You know he is not a very good shot, and so he has badly wounded without killing it."

"Then we ought to hear his gun again."

"We shall no doubt—"

"Hark!"

Crack went a gun, almost instantly followed by three similar reports. The boys turned pale and looked at each other.

"What does that mean?" whispered Elwood.

"That is bad; Tim is in trouble."

"He ought to have had better sense than to paddle out there in open day, plunge right into the woods and go to shooting without stopping to see what the danger is. But what will become of him?"

"And of us?"

"This Indian here must have had some way of getting upon the island. I believe he has a canoe hid somewhere."

"But what of it? We cannot think of leaving until we know

Edward S. Ellis

something definite about Tim."

"Unless some of the Indians start to come over to the island, and then we'll leave."

"Do you think that would be the wisest plan, Elwood? They can handle the paddle so much better than we that it would take but little time for them to overhaul us. Then, too, if they should find us by this suffering brother of theirs would it not make friends of them?"

"Suppose this Indian here is one of their enemies?"

This was a supposition that had never occurred to Howard before, but which he saw was very reasonable. All Indians not belonging to the same tribe might be supposed to be enemies of each other, and thus the mercy and kindness of our young heroes might be made the means of their destruction.

"I didn't think of that," said Howard, "it may be so. But let us hope for the best. Tim may soon return to us again."

"Not if he has a grain of sense left."

"And why not?"

"He has been seen by Indians, and if they haven't got him now they will soon have him if he undertakes to paddle his canoe over to the island."

"You are right, Elwood; he will no doubt wait until it is dark, and then come out to us as stealthily as he can."

"That is if he gets the chance. I tell you, Howard," said his cousin, starting up, "this begins to look bad."

"I know it does."

"We know how those red men handle their guns, and it don't look likely to me that all those shots have missed Tim."

"They may be quite a distance apart—far enough to make their aim uncertain."

"But then they could cut off his return to the shore."

Howard suddenly laid his hand upon the arm of his cousin and pointed to the other shore.

# CHAPTER XXII

## DANGER

Three Indians walked leisurely down to the shore of the river, as though in quest of nothing particular, and stood gesticulating as they generally do with their whole arms. They were about two hundred yards above the point where Tim O'Rooney landed, but their position was such that the canoe might have rested on the surface of the water without being seen. Sensible of their danger, the boys at first sight of them withdrew into cover, from which they cautiously peered out and watched their movements.

"Those must be the three who fired the guns," whispered Elwood.

"Very probably they are; that looks more encouraging, for I do not see Tim among them."

"Maybe they have slain him and are talking as to where he came from."

"Heaven! I hope not."

"So do I; but it looks reasonable that they have made away with him and are now looking for us."

"How did they know he had any friends with him? Then, too, if they had slain him, would they not have followed his trail straight down to the water?"

"I didn't think of that. *That* question makes me more hopeful than anything else. It does now look somewhat cheering. But what are they after?"

The Indians were still talking in an excited manner, and more than once pointed across the river to the island as if there were something there which claimed their attention. It might be the boys themselves, or they may have known that one of their race lay there in dire extremity; but whatever the cause was it boded no good to the two boys, who were crouching in the bushes and grass and furtively watching their motions.

The latter were still gazing at them when their hearts were thrilled by the sight of Tim O'Rooney. The eyes of Elwood chanced to be fixed upon a small open space, a rod or two from where the canoe lay, when he saw the Irishman come cautiously into view, and then pause and look around him. He had an animal slung over his shoulders, whose weight was sufficient to make him stop and travel with some difficulty. They saw him turn his head and carefully scrutinize every suspicious point that was visible, and then he walked slowly toward the spot where the canoe was concealed. Whether his low stoop was caused by the weight of his game, or whether it was a precautionary measure on his part, was difficult to decide. The boys at once became painfully excited and alarmed.

"They will see him! they will see him!" said Elwood, "and it will be all over with us. What a pity! when he has got along so well!"

"Can we not warn him in some manner? The Indians do not

know how near he is, nor does he know how close they are."

"How can we do it?" asked Elwood, who was anxious to give Tim some warning of his danger. "If we make any sign the Indians will see us."

"Perhaps not; for they are not looking in this direction all the time, while Tim knows that we are watching him."

"Yes; but he has his hands full to see that the savages do not find him."

The case looked critical indeed. Tim was nearing the point where it seemed inevitable that a discovery should take place. He paused at nearly every step or two, looked behind him and up and down the river in a manner that showed plainly enough his fear of his enemies. Elwood Brandon in his eagerness had risen to his feet, and was looking intently at him, waiting until he should cast his eye toward the island that he might give him warning. But the Irishman was so occupied with his enemies that he appeared to forget the existence of his friends.

Elwood did not remove his gaze, and all at once he saw him raise his head. Quick as a flash the boy sprung up a foot or two from the ground and waved his hat toward him.

"Did he see me?" he asked, as he sunk down to the earth again.

"He has paused and is looking toward us."

Tim had caught sight of the signal of the boy, but was uncertain as to its meaning. The waving of the hat might be supposed as an act of encouragement than otherwise; but there was something in the silent, hurried manner of his young friend, united with the fact that he had been, and was still, in great personal peril, that arrested his attention and set him to thinking.

"Did the Indians see me?" asked Elwood.

"I can't say positively, as I was looking at Tim at the moment you made your signal, but they do not seem to act as if they had discovered us."

"Tim saw me, didn't he? He doesn't know what to make of it."

The Irishman had laid the animal he was carrying upon the ground, and stood looking toward the inland as if waiting for some further manifestation before advancing or retreating. Believing the safety of the entire party demanded it, Elwood begun cautiously rising to his feet to repeat his warning, when he was quickly caught by his cousin.

"Down! those Indians are suspicious; they are looking right at us—don't stir."

The admonition was not a moment too soon; but while it prevented discovery on the part of the boys, it rendered the signal already given the Irishman void and of no effect. Tim, seeing nothing more of his young friend, concluded that all was right, and lifting his game to his shoulder continued his descent until he reached his canoe. This was drawn from its hiding place and launched in the water, and the animal placed in the rear. Seating himself carefully in the front, Tim lifted his paddle and began making his way toward the inland.

"Too bad! too bad!" muttered Elwood, unable to repress his feelings. "He is coming right out where they will have a fair chance with their rifles."

"If he would only turn up stream, they would see nothing of him."

"*Can't* I warn him?"

"No, Elwood, it will make matters worse. Their eyes are fixed upon us."

Grasping the long oar Tim headed his boat somewhat up stream, so as not to let it drift by the island, and commenced paddling across. He had gone twenty rods or thereabouts when he was discovered by the Indians, and one of them raised his rifle and took aim at him.

"Quick, Tim, drop down, or you'll be shot!" called out Howard, forgetful of his own danger in the single hope of saving his friend from a violent death.

At the same instant that this cry was uttered the terrified boy saw a puff of smoke issue from the Indian rifle, and simultaneous with the sharp crack Tim O'Rooney was seen to fall flat in the canoe.

"He is shot!" called out Elwood.

"It is time then for us to do some of the same kind of business," replied Howard, sighting his own gun at the savage upon the shore. The distance was too great and his skill too slight to guide the ball with anything like certainty, but it skipped over the water at their very feet, and so alarmed them that they immediately dodged back under the shelter of the rocks and trees.

"What is the use?" asked Elwood gloomily. "Poor Tim is killed and there is no chance for us."

"Look! he is not dead!" whispered Howard.

The head of the Irishman was seen to rise stealthily from the bottom of the canoe, and to peer around, and then to dash down again as though fearful of another shot.

"I don't believe he has been struck!" added Howard. "He dropped down so as to save himself."

"Oh! I hope so, for we need him bad enough. See! he is fixing the body of the animal so that it shall be between him and the Indians' guns."

Such was the case. Tim was arranging and placing the carcass so that it might shield his own body while he managed the paddle. This completed he turned his face toward his young friends and called across the water:

"Be aisy, me darlings! The owld bullet come close, but not a hair of Tim O'Rooney's head was touched, and thanks be to heaven for it!"

# CHAPTER XXIII

## DRIFTING AWAY

The bullet of the treacherous Indian had indeed whizzed harmlessly by the head of Tim O'Rooney and when he fell to the bottom of the canoe it was for the purpose of preventing any more of their missiles passing too near him.

The savages, hastily driven to shelter by the unexpected shot from the island, did not by any means relinquish their designs upon the unfortunate white man in the canoe. He who had taken the quick aim and fired saw that his bullet missed, but he understood the disadvantage of his enemy, and was confident that he would still fall into their hands.

As we have shown, when the Irishman was thus suddenly interrupted, he was but a short distance from the shore. So abruptly compelled to relinquish his paddle and simply shelter his person, the current carried him quite rapidly down the stream.

Tim did not become sensible of his disadvantage until he had drifted below the island, and then upon partly rising to use his paddle the crack of a gun from the shore told him that he was watched by vigilant eyes, and that *that* occupation was vetoed most unmistakably.

Forced thus to act entirely on the defensive, he carefully drew out his rifle and resting it on the body of his game waited his chance to avenge himself upon the unrelenting savages. He could tell from the faint blue smoke that curled upward where they were concealed, but could not catch sight of them.

Had they shown themselves, the Irishman knew it was about impossible for him to harm them at such a distance, while their dexterity in the use of the gun made it too dangerous for him to expose himself to their fire. He watched them until he had floated quite a way below, when he began to hope that they had given up their designs upon him, and he might make his way back to his friends upon the island in safety.

But when on the point of rising to a sitting position he saw them whisk through the bushes he knew they were following him along the shore—following him, too, with that skill and stealth which prevented his getting a shot at them, and placing it totally out of his power to prevent himself from being "commanded by their fire."

As may well be imagined, Howard and Elwood were deeply interested spectators of these events. Now that they had revealed their presence upon the island, and there was no further use in attempting to conceal the fact, they were eager to render their companion all the assistance possible.

But the nature of the occurrences made them helpless. Tim had drifted such a distance down stream, and had consequently drawn his enemies so far after him, that they had not the slightest chance of reaching them with their rifles, if they chose to expose themselves. They could only watch, therefore, and pray for their safety.

Floating slowly onward, onward, they observed that Tim's

Edward S. Ellis

canoe gradually swerved to the left until it disappeared around a curve in the river. It crossed the center and was nearer the western than the eastern shore. This seemed to show that, despite his unfavorable situation, he was able to impart a motion to the boat, which, slight as it was, would eventually bring him to the opposite side of the stream.

Nothing more was seen of the Indians, although the report of several guns, heard within a half-hour of the disappearance of the canoe, prevented their feeling too sanguine over the position of Tim O'Rooney.

"We can now see the blunder he committed," said Howard. "He did wrong in going to the eastern bank when he could have secured his game as well upon the other side."

"I think he will be able to get away, unless they have a canoe with which to follow him."

"Even then he can take to the woods and hide himself until dark, and then make his way back to us."

"I hope so, but fear he will be prevented or overtaken before he can reach shelter."

"But think, Howard, he has a gun and plenty of ammunition, and there are but three of them. I should say they would hesitate some time before advancing upon him."

"But he is a poor shot, like ourselves."

"He could not miss them if they came very close to him."

"Yes; there seems to be a good chance, if they don't find more Indians to unite with them in the hunt."

This was a contingency that had not occurred to Elwood, and he was almost overwhelmed at its import until he came to reason upon it, when the likelihood of such being the case dwindled away until it almost vanished.

"We have seen no large bodies of savages, and I don't believe they care enough about catching or slaying a single man to go to all that trouble."

"Not so much trouble, perhaps, as you are apt to think. War is the business of the American Indians, you know, as it is of all barbarous people."

"But look at Ned Trimble and his friends. There are but three of them, and I have no doubt that their security is in their strength—otherwise they would not be so indifferent as to what is going on around them. You remember they did not see us until we first spoke to them."

"So it appeared; but I have an idea that they knew of our presence before Tim discovered them."

"They did not show it, at any rate."

"They looked surprised when we came up, but if we had been enemies instead of friends I believe we would have been the surprised parties. They have lived too long in the wilds of California to permit a party of strangers to steal upon them unaware."

"But what is to become of us if Tim doesn't come back?"

"We shall have to put ourselves under the care of Shasta—that is, if he gets well."

"Why do you call him *Shasta*? Where did you hear that name?"

Edward S. Ellis

"The only word I have heard him speak sounded like that, and I do not know of any better name. Can you think of one?"

"No; that is good enough; let him be called Shasta, then. There may be a greater Providence in our coming upon this island than we imagine."

"There is a Providence in everything that occurs, though it may be that we are not always able to see it. Do you remember the copy we had so often at school, 'Misfortunes are often blessings in disguise?'"

"Yes; but like the truths that were driven into our heads so often at school, we fail to appreciate them until some occasion like this impresses them upon our minds. But I declare, Howard, we are turning philosophers."

"What better can we do, when there is nothing else to employ ourselves about? We need all our philosophy at such a time."

"But we must not forget our patient, Shasta."

"True. He had gone almost out of my mind until you referred to him a moment ago. Let us look at him."

The two had been stationed near the lower end of the island, and they now walked back to where they had left the suffering stranger. What was their surprise to see him standing on his feet, his blanket wrapped around him, and his attitude and position such as to raise a strong suspicion that he understood all that had taken place within the last hour or two.

# CHAPTER XXIV

## A HUNT

When Tim O'Rooney left the island and crossed to the eastern shore of the Salinas he had almost forgotten the existence of any such thing as hostile Indians. He was after something to eat, and some how or other it seemed to him that the climate of California had given him a most ravenous appetite, which demanded satisfaction regardless of consequences.

Touching land, he pulled his canoe up the bank to prevent its being carried away by the current, and then plunged boldly into the forest. The land from the river rose quite rapidly until it reached an elevation of several hundred feet, when it was broken by gorges, ravines and chasms, which made it rattier difficult to travel, and gave it an extremely wild and picturesque appearance.

Fairly among these broken hills, Tim began to look for his game, but for a time saw nothing to draw his fire. Finally he reached a wild-looking gorge which descended over a hundred feet below him, while upon the opposite side it rose to a greater height than the place upon which he stood.

The Irishman was so struck with the wild scenery that he

　　　　　　　Edward S. Ellis

stood a few moments contemplating it in silent admiration, when all at once he became conscious that something else beside himself was engaged in looking. Directly across the gorge, so as to be almost opposite to him, he saw the head of an animal which he recognized at once as belonging to a black-tailed deer.

"Be the powers! but you're jist the gintleman that I'd like to make an acquaintance with, as me mither said when me father axed her hand in marriage."

Tim drew his rifle carefully and rested it upon a rock beside him. The deer gazed at him with that expression of stupid wonder which wild animals assume when confronted with something, and they seem to be debating with themselves whether to leap away at high speed or to stare a moment longer.

The distance was so slight that Tim was sure of his aim. Nevertheless, he took great care in sighting his piece, and as his finger gently pressed the trigger, he held his breath. The bullet sped true, entering just below and between the eyes, and with such deadly effect that the mortally wounded deer sprung several feet in the air and fell dead within a rod of the spot where it had stood when struck.

"That is plaisant," muttered the Irishman, as he saw the animal fall, "and yez hav the distinguished honor of baing the first deer that Tim O'Rooney brought down; but yez ain't the first he fired at—but whist, Tim, don't be telling your secrets, for somebody else might larn them."

He now began making his way carefully down the gorge in order to ascend upon the opposite side and secure his prize. He had no thought that the report of his gun could reach the ears of hostile persons, and he did not heed anything except the place and manner in which he put his feet in going down and up the ravine.

After no little toiling he reached the dead body, and found that he had shot a rather small black-tailed deer. It was in middling condition, and was the very prize he was anxious to secure for his hungry self and equally hungry friends.

As he stood admiring it, for the first time the thought of personal danger crossed his mind, and he glanced hurriedly around him, but saw nothing to occasion alarm. Then he leaned forward and gazed down the gorge, and as he did so he descried three Indians looking up the side of the chasm. Slight as was the distance his head projected, it was seen by them, and he only drew it back to escape the effect of three discharges of their guns.

"And that is your shtyle of saluting a gintleman is it?" said Tim in some trepidation. "But yez has a forcible way of saying 'how do yez do,' in this counthry, that a stranger would do well to imitate."

The Irishman hastily debated with himself upon the best plan to pursue to escape the serious peril that threatened him, for he was sure the savages would follow up their shot.

"The best thing I can do is to lave," he concluded. "There is strong raison for belaving that I've given some one slight offinse by walking into their house without ringing the bell."

He stooped over and lifted his game. He found its weight somewhat less than he had suspected.

"I have no objiction to your going wid me. If I has to have the same dispute about ivery deer I tips over, I may as well hang on to the fust one."

Slinging it over his shoulder, he began his return with the carcass. It proved beneficial to him in a way that he had little suspected. Not wishing to go any further down the gorge, where there was reason to fear a collision with the savages, he clambered still higher, taking great care to shield himself from observation from below.

This made his labor excessive, and he was often obliged to pause and rest himself. But at length he reached what might be termed the brow of the hill, and began making his way along the edge of a smaller ravine, that led toward the river. While thus engaged, the body of the deer struck a projecting rock, and before Tim could save himself he rolled over and over for a distance of twenty odd feet, coming down plump upon the deer without injuring himself in the least.

"I'm obliged to yez," he said, as he rose and stared around with a bewildered air. "That was kind in yez, and I'll not forget the favor."

Again raising his carcass to his shoulder, he resumed his journey toward the river. But as he progressed the weight upon his shoulder seemed to grow heavier, and he was obliged to pause and rest himself quite often. On these occasions he looked around him half-expecting to see the three savages spring out of the bushes.

If such a thing should occur, Tim had already decided upon his mode of procedure. He intended to sink to the ground at once, with the body of the deer as a sheltering breastwork, and make as gallant fight as possible. His success in bringing down his game, when it was fully fifty yards distant, gave him quite a flattering estimate of his prowess.

The Indians, as the Irishman had anticipated, hastened up the gorge to secure the daring hunter, who had so audaciously exposed himself to their anger. It required some time for them to find the exact spot where the deer had fallen, and when they did so, they followed him readily by the blood which had trickled from its drooping head, which as Tim bore his prize away he little dreamed would betray the course he took.

When the point of Tim's fall was reached, all signs of his trail ceased, and they supposed he had checked the flow of blood, and thus concealed his tracks. The surface over which he traversed being rock and flinty ground, left no evidence of his passage; and resigning, therefore, the pursuit in this manner, they made their way leisurely down to the river and waited until the hunter appeared.

Tim's heart beat high with hope when he found himself close by the stream and saw nothing of his pursuers. The hasty signal given by Elwood Brandon, as we have shown, caused him some uneasiness, but not being repeated, and being very anxious to get back to the island, he placed the deer in the canoe and paddled away.

# CHAPTER XXV

## A SINGULAR ESCAPE

The shot from the treacherous Indian upon the shore was the first intelligent warning Tim had that he was discovered by them. The kind Providence who had so often turned aside the dangerous missile still protected him, and when he so suddenly dropped to the bottom of his canoe, it was with a bullet-hole through his coat but not through his body.

"Another illigant compliment to mesilf that it would afford me great pleasure to return, and if you'll only be kind enough to wait a few moments, I'll do the same."

But ere he could bring his gun to bear, the wild shot from the island drove the savages to cover, and raised the Irishman's finger that was pressing the trigger.

We have already told how, when he undertook to use the paddle, he found it too dangerous, and coming again behind the deer, he floated down the current. This, after the severe labor he had undergone, was an agreeable change, but he was not long in discovering it was dangerous. He was drifting away from his friends, and the further he went the greater did the danger become to both parties. He speedily discovered that the Indians were following him, and the interposing body of the black-tailed deer was a most effectual protection. More than his own bullets were buried in it ere he had gone a half-mile down stream.

"If I entertained a small doubt that yez was killed, I couldn't howld it with them bullets rattlin' in your hide, me owld friend."

The efforts of a child, if steadily persevered in, would move the Great Eastern in calm water, and Tim was not long in making the discovery that, if he could not use the paddle, he still was able to exert a motive power upon the canoe by a very slight means.

Reaching his hand over the side, he began paddling the water, and soon had the gratifying consciousness that he was moving across the river. True, it was slow, but it was nevertheless certain and positive, and was carrying him further away from his troublesome pursuers, and must eventually bring him against the western shore.

But when the island disappeared from view, and he had barely crossed the center of the stream, he begun to think that this species of locomotion was rather tardy, and he partially came to the sitting position and ventured to take his paddle in hand. A discharge from the shore warned him of the danger he ran, and he was reluctantly forced to drop his head again and resort to his tedious method of moving.

By this time the afternoon was well advanced, and it looked as though it would be fully dark before Tim could regain the ground he had lost. Now and then he peered over the top of the deer to see whether he could possibly catch sight of his acquaintances, but they whisked from cover to cover so dexterously that he had not the encouragement even to hope for success, and so he did not fire.

But a new fear took possession of the fugitive. If they were Indians, it was to be expected that they had canoes somewhere, and if they were speedily found, he would as speedily be overhauled.

"In which case Tim O'Rooney will lose his daar, and be the same towken lose himself, and the boys won't get their dinner."

He squinted at the sun, now low in the sky, and quickly asked himself:

"If a man doesn't git his dinner, and ates half-way atween noon and midnight, is it his dinner or supper? But that is a mighty question, is the same."

He evidently concluded it was too vast for him to decide, for he speedily dismissed it and turned his attention to that which more nearly concerned him. Still toiling with his hand, much in the same manner that a child would dabble in the water, he kept up the tardy movement of the canoe until he began to grow fearless again, and he took his paddle once more.

Now, when it was almost too late, he found that he could use it without danger to himself. By bending his body forward, the deer protected him and he could labor with impunity.

"Tim O'Rooney, I fears yez are lacking in the iliments which go to make up a mon of sense. Why didn't yez think of this when it would have done yez more good?"

When he was yet within a few yards of shore, he looked back and was not a little frightened to see that the savages had launched a canoe and were coming across the river with the speed of the swallow.

"Whisht now! but that is onexpected," said he, as he redoubled his own exertions. Observing that his pursuers were rapidly gaining, he suddenly recalled an artifice that he had seen practiced during his experience in the mines years before. Catching up his rifle, he aimed it at the advancing Indians.

Quick as a flash they ducked their heads and held up the two paddles they were using as a protection against the expected bullet. But it was not Tim's purpose to fire. He knew better than to do that, for ere he could have reloaded they would have been upon him.

The minute they stooped he lowered his gun and caught up his paddle and used it furiously. In this he was imitated by the Indians, whose superior skill sent their frail vessel forward with such velocity that it looked as if they would reach the shore but a short distance behind him.

Again he raised his gun, and as before they attempted to screen themselves from danger, while the next impulse of his paddle sent his canoe high up the bank, and he sprung out and plunged into the woods.

Tim O'Rooney had no thought of the particular manner in which he was to effect his escape. His one desire was to get away from them. The probabilities are that, beyond all doubt, he would have been speedily overtaken and slain but for one of those singular occurrences which do not happen to a man more than once in a life-time, and which seem to show unmistakably that Providence often interferes directly in favor of the innocent and distressed.

He had run perhaps a couple of hundred yards, or thereabouts, when a peculiar whoop from his pursuers announced that they had landed and were now coming speedily behind him. He knew that he had no chance in running, and was looking about him for some place in which to take shelter, when a furious growl startled him and he found himself within a dozen feet from enormous grizzly bear. This quadruped seemed anxious for a fight, for he came straight at the fugitive, who might certainly be excused for being dazed at the combination of dangers by which he was surrounded.

That of the grizzly bear was the greatest; for with mouth open and his red tongue lolling out he came fiercely at him. His gait was awkward and shambling, but he managed to get over the ground very rapidly. Indeed, the danger was so imminent that Tim, seeing there was no choice, raised his gun and fired at the monster.

The bullet struck him near the head, but it did not kill him, nor did it cause him to fall, but it bewildered him, and he rose on his hind feet and clawed the air as if the bullet was a splinter and he was seeking to pluck it from his flesh.

This bewilderment was the means of Tim being saved. Before the animal had entirely recovered, he had darted out of sight, and when the Indians came up the bear was just in "fighting trim," and immediately made at them. Consequently they were compelled to give over all thoughts of the flying hunter and attend to their own personal safety. What the final result was Tim never learned, and we cannot speak with certainty.

# CHAPTER XXVI

## SHASTA'S HUNT

If the Pah Utah in the extremity of his suffering had been betrayed into the extraordinary weakness of manifesting it, he now seemed anxious to make amends for the humiliating fact. It may have been that among his own people he would have restrained those utterances which declared his agony, and borne the utmost with the stoicism of his race; but knowing that civilization does not teach such outward indifference to pain, he had adopted the surest means to reach the sympathy of the white strangers; or, if we may conjecture still further, the consciousness of the instinctive feud between the American and Caucasian race told him that the plan he took was the only one that offered safety to himself. What reason had he to believe that the hunters were kind of heart? If he hid his distress, would he not be treated as a well Indian? And was there any but the one common ground upon which the two races met?

But the fever had passed and he was himself again. True, he was still feeble, and his limbs trembled at times like those of an old man; but the disease had gone, and the stern, unbending will had resumed its sway. He was not a child, but he was Shasta, the Pah Utah Indian.

Edward S. Ellis

The inexperience of Elwood Brandon and Howard Lawrence with these strange people made this savage an enigma to them. As he stood with his arms folded, his blanket wrapped around him, his long black hair streaming over his shoulders, and the mingling of the paint on his crown and over his face, and his midnight eyes fixed upon them, it was hard indeed to conjecture the thoughts filtrating through his brain.

But there is a language in which the human heart can speak— that of emotion. The boys felt no fear—ingratitude is not an element of the savage character, though sad to say it is sometimes manifested among us of greater moral pretensions.

He looked at them as they came up and paused a few feet from him.

"You seem to be better?" asked Elwood, feeling it incumbent that he should make some remark, even though it was incomprehensible to their dusky friend. He muttered something and then stretched out his arms as if to show that he had recovered from his illness.

At this point Terror went up to the savage and snuffed around him, as if to satisfy himself of his identity. The latter laid his hand upon his knife and watched the dog narrowly, but he appeared to judge the animal by the company, and quietly removed his hand and folded his arms again.

He stood thus a moment, when he pointed to the eastern shore and then down the river, nodding his head and gesticulating somewhat excitedly. The boys in return nodded, which satisfied the aborigine. All at once he moved off and strode rapidly to the other side of the island, where he drew forth a tiny canoe and shoved it into the water.

When it was launched he turned again toward his friends,

and looking steadily at them a moment, once more pointed down stream, sprang into the boat and dipped his paddle first upon one side and then upon the other.

It was a sight to see him manage the canoe! It seemed made to contain a single person, and the way it skimmed over the water was a perfect marvel to the spectators. It appeared fairly to fly, scarcely touching the water, while human art could not have exceeded the skill with which he managed the paddle. He sat as motionless as a statue, like the artistic violinist. It could not be seen that he raised his arms above the elbow.

The sun was just going over the western hills, and the reflection of the water as it flashed and rippled from his paddle gave a fairy-like appearance to the Indian as he sped down stream that was pleasing to the last degree.

"What does that mean?" asked Elwood.

"It means that he is going to the rescue of Tim."

"If he goes after him he will bring him back. Just see the way in which he manages that canoe! It is worth going a hundred miles to see!"

"No doubt he has practiced it long enough."

"But what of our remaining here?"

"I don't see how it can be helped."

"Suppose those Indians that have followed Tim take it into their heads to pay us a visit?"

"He will take all their attention, if Shasta concludes to have a

Edward S. Ellis

part in the matter, and they won't have time to think of us."

"But suppose they *do* come back here?"

"We must be prepared at any rate; but don't let the thought make us uneasy. We have two good guns, and Terror would be worth half a dozen men if we get into close quarters."

"He may be all that; but a rifle-shot could quickly stretch him out lifeless. It won't do for us to go to sleep until Tim or Shasta come back."

"Of course not. I do not feel like it, even if we were satisfied that it was safe for us to do so."

"Look at Shasta!"

The Indian was far down the stream, still speeding with his extraordinary velocity, using his arms as though they would never tire.

"So sick a few hours ago!"

"Well enough now."

"Didn't you notice how he trembled?"

"Yes; he is still weak, but an Indian soon recovers himself."

"All he needed was the root which he chewed and which cured him almost immediately. These savages are what you call Thomsonians I suppose."

"They are the original ones no doubt. I have heard that some of their medicine men are the most skillful of physicians."

"Yes; we hear all kinds of things about them. What stories we have read, and yet they don't look and act as I imagined they would. I thought they would suffer and die without showing the least pain, and yet Shasta wasn't anyways backward about it."

"No doubt the poor fellow felt bad enough, and he hasn't got over it yet. You can tell that from his appearance."

"It will take all his skill to help Tim. Just as like as not he will take Shasta for an enemy and shoot him."

"If they only see each other before dark, so that Tim can understand that he has a friend at work."

"But you see it is nearly dark now, and it is likely he is in the woods by this time."

"What danger can he be in then?"

"The Indians may cross over to follow him."

They were silent a while when Elwood suddenly exclaimed.

"Suppose Shasta is an enemy and has gone to help his people?"

Howard shook his head.

"No fear of that. That is the last thing that can occur."

The night gradually deepened and proved to be quite dark, a faint moon shedding a luster that made the dim light more impressive. The boys walked back and forth, watching and listening for some evidence of the approach of their friends, and gradually becoming apprehensive despite the attempt each made to cheer the spirits of the other.

It was not until quite late that Terror gave utterance to a low, warning growl, and as they looked across the river they descried a dark object cautiously approaching.

"What is it?" whispered Elwood.

"It is too dark to tell; but it can't be Tim or Shasta for it's coming from the wrong direction."

"Aisy now, Mr. Shasta, aisy I say, for the boys may be asleep and we won't come upon them too sudden't like, as me uncle said when he sat on a barrel of gun-powder and it blowed up with him. Aisy, Mr. Shasta, aisy!"

# CHAPTER XXVII

## THE NIGHT VOYAGE

The indistinct object gradually took shape, and the boys then saw Shasta sitting in his small canoe, while directly behind him was Tim O'Rooney, his left hand extended backward and grasping the prow of his own boat, which was being towed by the Indian.

The next moment the foremost lightly touched the shore and the savage sprung out, quickly followed by the Irishman.

"I beg yez pardon, boys, for the time I tuk to git your dinner; but to shpake the thruth, I was unavoidably detained, as me brother writ me when he was locked up in Tipperary jail on his way to visit me."

"We are glad enough to see you again, but where is your game?"

"Worrah, worrah, but I had bad luck wid it. When I tuk it ashore, I sat it down for a minit, and I hadn't the time to pick it up again."

"But tell us all about it."

Edward S. Ellis

This was quickly done, up to the point where Tim was saved by the timely appearance of the grizzly bear, when, as may well be supposed, the expressions of wonder were loud and continued.

"You saw nothing more of your pursuers?" asked Howard.

"Not a bit—nor be the same towken do I think they saw me."

"How did you and Shasta meet?"

"That was shtrange, was the same. After I found I was cl'ar of the varmints, from the raisin that their exclusive attention was occupied by the b'ar, I stopped and went to thinking— did I. I could saa the great necessity of our having me own canoe and I went back to whom I left the same. It took me some time to find it, and when I did find it, it wasn't it, but the one that belonged to the red gintlemen.

"There was little difference atwixt the two and I thought the best thing was to make a thrade, and just as I thought that I spied another canoe coming along the shore as though it was looking for something. I stepped back and raised the hammer of my gun, when I obsarved there was but one Injin in the same—was there. So, 'Tim,' says I, "twould be a shame,' and I lowered me gun agin.

"Just then, and fur the life of me I don't know what put it into me head, I thought it was Shasta, though I knowed I had lift him with a big pain all through him. So I give a low whistle like, and called out 'Shasta,' and with one whip of his paddle he sent his canoe right at my faat, though I was sure he didn't saa me, and then waited fur me to step in.

"But he's a quaar fellow, is Shasta," added Tim. "I rached out me hand to shake his own, but he never noticed it, but motioned fur me to stow mesilf into the bottom of the canoe; and thin, after some muttering and throwing of his arms, I could saa he wanted me to howld on to the other canoe."

"And I did the same, and the way he towed us over the water would have frightened a steamboat."

"He is a smart fellow, indeed."

The Indian upon landing had just pulled his canoe slightly up the bank and then had gone at once to the opposite side of the island where he had lain when sick. They could see him walking slowly back and forth us if searching for something which he had some difficulty in finding.

"Well, boys, I shpose you are hungry," said Tim, "If yez isn't I begins to howld a very strong suspicion that it's meself that is."

"Yes," replied Elwood, "we are both very hungry, but we had little appetite so long as we knew you were in danger."

"It was very kind of yez to restrain your appetite out of respict to me, and I'll not forgit to do the same when yez git into throuble."

"We can afford to go supperless to-night," remarked Howard, "and feast on the contemplation of our good fortune. There was a time when our prospects looked pretty dark."

"Yis, sir; you may well say that. When I had the big bear walking at me from one direction and the three red gintlemen from the other, I thought to mesilf what a shplendid opportunity there was for the illigant exercise of one's idaas. But it was all the doings of the good Lord above," added Tim very reverently.

"Yes; there can be no doubt of that," replied Howard. "He has cared for us all the time."

Tim now gave an account of his adventures in his hunt after the deer, previous to when he was first seen from the island. When he had finished Elwood asked:

"Are we to stay here over night?"

"I think not, but I defers to the judgment of Mr. Shasta. It's just as he says about it."

"He appears to be taken up with something over yonder."

"He is searching for some object that he left when he made up his mind to get well," said Howard.

"He must know all that has occurred, for when we came back from watching you, there he stood with his arms folded, and a look in his eye that said he understood more about matters and things than we imagined he did."

"He must know that we are in danger so long as we are upon this island, and I should think he would leave it while it is dark.'"

"Do yez rest on that pint?" said Tim. "The red gintlemen will attind to the same—will he."

At this juncture the Pah Utah was observed walking slowly toward them, his long blanket grasped at the breast by his left hand, while his right was free. As soon as he came up he pointed at the canoes and muttered something.

"What does he mean?" asked Elwood.

"Terror understands him better than we do," replied Howard, as the Newfoundland sprung into the larger boat and nestled down near the stern.

Our friends were not long in imitating the action of the dog. Tim made as if to step into the Indian's boat, but he motioned him back, and took his seat in the front of the larger canoe. The savage now produced a cord, probably the tendon of some wild animal, with which he speedily fastened the prow of the larger canoe to the stem of his own.

This done he turned the head down stream and began using his paddle with the same wonderful dexterity he had displayed during the afternoon. The boys watched and admired his skill for a long time. The faint moon barely revealed the shores on either hand, stretching away in misty gloom, while all before and behind them was darkness.

The muscular arms of Shasta appeared to be as tireless as the piston-rods of an engine, and at last our friends grow weary of watching him. The boys became drowsy, and they finally lay down in the bottom of the boat, with their blanket over them, and went to sleep.

In the course of an hour Tim did the same, and the Pah Utah was this left alone to ply the canoe, the Newfoundland now and then raising his head and looking over the edge as if to satisfy himself that all was right.

Once near the middle of the night Elwood awoke, and pushing his blanket from his face, raised himself on his elbow and looked around. The same picture met his eye—the dark-hued Shasta, his long hair streaming over his shoulders, the blanket down to his waist, and his bronzed arms working with the silence, skill and regularity of a perfect machine.

Edward S. Ellis

# CHAPTER XXVIII

## A PAH UTAH'S METHOD OF FISHING

The gray light of dawn was spreading over the wood and river when Elwood Brandon again opened his eyes. He was somewhat startled to see nothing of the Pah Utah, although his canoe was still in the advance; but a second look showed that they were resting against the bank, and the Indian lay asleep in the front of his boat, his body and face covered entirely by his somber-hued blanket.

"No doubt he needs rest, and so I will not wake him!" was Elwood's thought, as he carefully raised himself to the sitting position. But he had scarcely moved when the end of Shasta's blanket was raised, and the boy saw his dark eyes fixed inquiringly upon him. Satisfied that there was nothing wrong the blanket dropped again and all was still.

Elwood now looked around. Howard was sleeping soundly, his feet resting against the shaggy sides of Terror, who was equally oblivious to the external world. There could be no doubt of Tim's somnolence for he gave unmistakable evidence of it. The light was just sufficient to afford a distinct view of the other shore, and in the clear summer air of the morning it had a cool appearance, very pleasing and refreshing to the eye.

Elwood, of course, had no knowledge of the distance they had come during the night; but he believed Shasta had not slept more than an hour or two, and that as a consequence they were many miles from their starting point—far enough at any rate to make them perfectly easy regarding the troublesome visitors of yesterday.

He noticed the peculiar character of the place in which Shasta had run the canoe. It was a small indentation covered with overhanging limbs and shrubbery in such manner that while the whites could peer out upon the river there was no danger of their being seen by any passers-by, unless particular suspicion was directed toward the spot.

Elwood's limbs were so cramped from the forced position in which he had lain during the night, that he concluded there could be no harm in stepping ashore to yawn and stretch himself. Of course he would take good care not to wander away from the boat, as he had seen the danger of secession in a small party like theirs. As he was stepping over the canoe he saw Shasta looking at him so intently that he paused. The Pah Utah nodded, but made a rather odd gesture, which Elwood took as a caution not to wander away. He nodded assent and stepped out upon the land. At this juncture Howard awoke and followed him.

"Shall we try and hunt something for breakfast?" asked Elwood.

"Tim's troubles have proved that it is hardly safe; I think we had better leave all such matters to Shasta."

This was good advice certainly, and the boys acted upon it. They walked up and down the banks of the river admiring the beautiful scenery, but seeing nothing of wild animals. They heard the whirr of a flock of birds overhead, alarmed by the apparition of two human beings, but the luxuriant vegetation allowed but a glimpse of them as they shot away.

While a few rods distant, they heard the discharge of a rifle, and in no little trepidation they hastened back to their friends. They were relieved by finding that it had been done by Tim O'Rooney for the purpose of affording a means of ignition to some sticks and leaves. He and the Pah Utah were on shore, making as much preparation for their breakfast as though they had a dozen men to provide for.

"What does yez think of it?" asked Tim.

"All very well, but where is your breakfast?"

The Irishman jerked his thumb in a very significant manner toward Shasta.

"You don't mean to eat him," laughed Elwood.

"Git out wid yer nonsense!" retorted Tim. "He and meself have been talking together, and we've fixed the whole thing."

"What language did you use?"

"This kind of talk."

And the Irishman explained himself by several extravagant but meaningless gestures.

The fire being nicely burning, Shasta took some white crumbs from a sort of receptacle in his hunting-shirt, stepped carefully into the canoe, and then gently dropped them upon the surface of the water. Our friend watched his movements with interest.

Leaning carefully over the boat, he curved his arm and held his closed fingers so that they were just within the water, looking down into the stream all the time with the fixedness of gaze that characterizes the hawk when about to dart downward after his prey.

Suddenly a flight ripple was heard, and before either of the three on shore comprehended what he was doing, something flashed before their gaze, and a plump, glistening fish, fully two pounds in weight, lay floundering at their feet.

"Capital!" shouted Elwood in his excitement, and he was proceeding to pay the Pah Utah several highly flavored compliments, when he raised his hand as a warning for them to remain quiet. Bending still further over the canoe, he soon thrust his hand beneath, and with the same lightning-like quickness flung a still larger fish up the bank. This was continued for some time, until he had five fine plump-looking fellows all shining and fresh, waiting for the hungry stomachs.

They had an abundance of food, and its preparation now only remained. Here Shasta displayed his remarkable culinary skill. With his keen-edged hunting-knife he slitted the fish, excepting Terror's portion, which of course was devoured raw, the entire length of the bodies, and throwing aside the superfluous portion, then skewered them upon some green prongs in such a manner that they were completely flat, and the entire internal and external surface exposed.

The fire, which had been burning some time, was now raked down until several square feet of live red coals lay bare, when one of the fish was held down within a few inches. As soon as one side was thoroughly cooked the other was turned under, and after this same fashion the four were most speedily and thoroughly prepared for the palate.

Edward S. Ellis

"Luxurious!" exclaimed Howard, as he took his prize and buried his teeth in its flesh. "It is cooked to perfection—a trifle of pepper and salt would make this the best dish I ever tasted."

"I never enjoyed a meal more," replied Elwood. "But when I come to think, the first one I tasted in California was nearly as good as this."

Tim was too much engaged to take time for conversation. He waited until he had filled himself to repletion, when he gave a great sigh of relief and remarked:

"I ain't hungry—not a bit; I've lost me appetite very quickly. Mr. Shasta, you're an excellent cook—worthy of the honor of attending to the wants of Timothy O'Rooney, Esquire."

The Pah Utah paid no heed to this praise, but contented himself with devouring his fish, which he did until he had all that he wished, when from some hidden recess he produced a beautifully carved Indian pipe.

"There I'm wid yees agin," remarked Tim, as he replenished his own. "The pipe is very soothin' to one's faalings after sevare labor, as me brother's wife used to say after whacking a few hours wid her broomstick—what is your opinion upon the same, Mr. Shasta?"

The Indian nodded his head and murmured some unintelligible reply.

"Precisely," assented Tim, as he puffed forth a thick volume of smoke; "that's me own idaas exactly, and the boys here will bear me witness that I've always contended for the same."

"What's that?" asked Elwood.

"Ax him," replied Tin, nodding his head toward his dusky friend. "He's able to explain better nor is meself."

Edward S. Ellis

# CHAPTER XXIX

## A NIGHT DISTURBANCE

Neither the Pah Utah nor the Irishman were disposed to make a move until they had finished their "smoke," and both of them whiffed as leisurely as though they had contracted to spend several hours thus. Howard and Elwood passed the time in walking around the woods and along the stream, taking particular care not to go beyond sight of Shasta, whose black orbs they could see attentively following their movements.

"All aboard!" shouted Tim at the expiration of an hour or so, and the boys hurried down to the "wharf" with as much alacrity as if they had heard the last bell of the steamer.

The Indian stood upon the shore with a look of inquiry. He pointed up stream and then down.

"He is inquiring which way we wish to go," said Howard.

"That, is strange, after bringing us so many miles from the island."

Elwood pointed down stream, but Shasta was not satisfied; he wished to know something more. He described several circles, terminating each time by pointing to the north. All three looked inquiringly at one other's faces. They could not comprehend his meaning.

"What does he wish to say?"

"I am sure I cannot tell."

"He wants us to travel the rest of the way by turning summersits."

Seeing that he was not understood, the Pah Utah took the paddle from the canoe and made in the air as if he were impelling the boat, then pausing, he again pointed to the north, and took several long strides in that direction, as though he were going to walk a long distance.

Elwood's eyes sparkled.

"I know what, he means! I know what he means!"

"What is it?"

"He wishes to ask whether we want to *go a good ways*!"

"You are right," replied Howard. "He doesn't know whether we are hunting in these parts, and wish to stay in the neighborhood, or whether we are hurrying home as fast as we can."

Shasta's motions and signs were imitated as nearly as possible, and he nodded his head and muttered something doubtless to signify that he was satisfied. Terror whisked into the canoe and took his position in the prow, while his three masters, if a dog can own that many, arranged themselves behind him. The tendon still united the two boats,

Edward S. Ellis

and one sweep of Pah Utah's paddle sent the two far out into the river, where he began his work.

For a time our friends gave themselves up to the enjoyment of this pleasant motion. At each dip of the paddle, or contraction of the iron muscles of Shasta, they could feel the canoe jump forward as does a steamboat under the throbs of the mighty engine. At the same time the motion was light and airy, as if the boat were skimming over the very surface. Indeed, by shutting the eyes and feeling the light wind fanning the temples, it was easy to imagine that they were borne through the air by some great bird whose wings could be felt to pulsate beneath them.

"Look at that machinery!" exclaimed Howard. "Did you ever see anything like it? Not an ounce of superfluous flesh upon him. See how the muscles swell and ridge, and yet he doesn't swerve his body a hair's breadth to the right or left."

"He can 'paddle his own canoe,'" laughed Elwood.

"Look at those shoulders; they are perfect mountains of muscle, and those sinewy arm! His legs are fully as perfect, and I'll warrant he can run a dozen miles an hour for a whole day without getting tired. He would be a dangerous man to meet as an enemy."

"And a good one as a friend."

"Yes; I can hardly see what chances we would have had of reaching the mouth of the river without his help."

"We had no chance unless we could join a party of hunters and induce them to go with us."

"Boys," said Tim, looking hard at them, "it isn't right—isn't the same."

"What do you mean?"

"That Mr. Shasta should tow us along in this shtyle, and we sit in the owld boat and permit him. No, it's wrong."

The boys admitted that it looked hardly proper, whereupon Tim took the paddle and began plying it with all the skill of which he was master. The Pah Utah looked over his shoulder now and then with a strange expression, as if he were amused at the white man's furious efforts, but he did not abate his own labor in the least.

Tim O'Rooney made a great deal of splashing, occasionally flirting a shower of spray over his friends as the paddle took an unexpected twist in his hand; but, as we have said before, he had had considerable experience in propelling a canoe, and he gave a little assistance to their dusky friend.

When the sun was overhead, Shasta directed the prow of the boat toward the western bank, and they landed in a place somewhat resembling that of the morning. The boats were drawn upon land in the usual manner, by which they were concealed from the observation of any passing up or down stream.

The Indian resorted to the same means by which he had caught the fish in the morning and with equal success. They were rather smaller, but none the less savory, either to man or brute. An hour sufficed to rest them all, and to give Shasta all the pleasure of his pipe that he wished, while Tim continued his after entering the canoe. Howard and Elwood made an essay with the paddle, but the result with the latter was that the instant he so cautiously thrust it beneath the surface, it was suddenly wrung from his hand, and in an instant left a rod or two astern. This necessitated a delay in order to pick it up, and the boys concluded to await another time to perfect themselves in the art of managing an Indian canoe.

It was not until it was quite dark that they once more set foot upon land and kindled their fire. There was quite a strong wind blowing, and the chill of the air appeared to indicate that it came from the snowy peaks of the Coast Range. Fully an hour was taken in gathering wood, sticks, broken limbs and branches, for they had concluded to keep it burning until morning.

The fire was kindled against the trunk of a giant sycamore, and as the flames waved up the shaggy bark the reflection upon the outstretched limbs and neighboring trees gave them a weird appearance that made the boys gather close to the somber-hued Pah Utah as though conscious of his ability to stand between them and evil.

Tim and Shasta were leisurely smoking their pipes, and Howard and Elwood were conversing together in low tones of their homes and friends, when a quick bark from Terror, as he rose to his feet and looked in the darkness, drew all eyes in one direction. A score of flashing eyes, gleaming teeth, lank, restless bodies and greedy jaws announced, that a new danger threatened them.

# CHAPTER XXX

## THE WOLVERINES

The Pah Utah was the only member of the party that did not manifest any alarm or excitement. Carelessly removing his pipe from his mouth, he turned his head, looked at the animals a moment, and then resumed smoking, without giving utterance to a single sound or changing his posture in the least.

Tim O'Rooney, with an ejaculated prayer, caught up his rifle, and turning his back toward the fire, stood like a person driven at bay and waiting to decide in his mind the best way to strike his last blow. In his haste and alarm his pipe fell from his mouth and lay unheeded at his feet. Shasta quietly picked it up, handed it to him, and motioned for him to seat himself upon the ground again. Tim stared alternately at the animals, the Indian and his pipe, and finally gathered the idea that no imminent danger threatened them.

Howard and Elwood also held their rifles ready for it charge from the growling wolverines, for such they were, while the Newfoundland growled in turn, and glared defiantly at them. The intelligent brute appeared to comprehend that it would not do for him to sally out and charge upon the enemy's works, but he stood ready to fight and die in the defense of his friends.

"Why don't they attack us?" asked Elwood, seeing that they didn't advance nearer than a dozen feet.

"Don't you know that wild animals are afraid of fire? That is what restrains them."

"Of course! I didn't think of that. How fortunate that we gathered enough wood to last!"

"Just look at Shasta! He doesn't even stop smoking!"

"He must know there is no danger."

"Let us try our guns upon them!"

The proposal pleased both, especially as there was no fear but what they could make every discharge tell. Each of them singled out two of the largest wolverines, and fired their guns at the same instant. An ear-splitting clamor succeeded, and as the brutes scampered away in the darkness two of their number were seen stretched out, quivering and dying.

The wolverine is an animal found in California which unites the characteristics of the bear, weasel, fox and wolf. It is sullen and ferocious, and one of the most troublesome of the wood-denizens. When first seen it is apt to be mistaken for a small bear, or rather heavy-looking wolf. The sensuous neck and head bespeak the wolf and weasel nature, the sly persistency the fox, and the savage stubbornness that of the bear; while a resemblance to all four can be seen in the general contour, appearance and habits of the animal.

Attracted, no doubt, by the smell of the cooking fish, a number of these brutes had slyly gathered and crept to the camp, where, finding their prey protected by the fire, they proclaimed their furious disappointment by loud howls—half bark and half yell—springing hither and thither among each other, sometimes vaulting over each other's backs, and darting as close to the bristling dog as their mortal dread of the fire would permit.

Terror stood on the outskirts of the camp, occasionally moving forward toward the animals, as if to match his long white teeth and massive strength against their glittering fangs and treacherous ferocity.

When the two guns were discharged the rest disappeared as if a bombshell had exploded in their midst; but scarcely a dozed seconds elapsed ere they closed together again, fiercer and more clamorous, if possible, than before.

In a few moments the boys had their guns reloaded, and they immediately repeated their former proceeding with precisely the same result. At this point a surprising occurrence came to pass. The dead wolverines were pounced upon by their survivors and torn instantly to shreds, and even devoured with as much avidity as if they were Terror and his human companions.

"Did you ever hear of such a thing?" asked Elwood, watching them in great amazement.

"Yes; I have read of wolves doing the same, even when one of their number was not killed but only wounded slightly."

"Any animals that act in that manner deserve death; so let's send a few more rifle-balls among them."

"If we keep this up for a few hours I don't see that there will be any left, and we may rest in peace."

"They will keep on gathering until there are twice that number. If it wasn't for our fire we should have to take to the trees; and what, then, would become of poor Terror?"

"He will get into trouble as it is," said Howard, "if we don't keep an eye on him."

The dog had continued advancing closer to the wolverines, until there was an imminent probability of a collision occurring between him and two of the largest, that sprung forward until they were within a few inches of him, when they darted back again to repeat the feint, seemingly with the purpose of drawing the Newfoundland further toward their clutches.

Howard spoke sharply to Terror, but he paid no heed to the call. The boy repeated it with the same uselessness, and he was beginning to become seriously alarmed for his fate when Shasta laid down his pipe and rose to his feet. The eyes of the three were now centered upon him.

The Pah Utah left his gun and blanket upon the ground, so that his arms and breast, excepting a few ornaments, were bare. He then drew his keen hunting-knife and held it rigidly grasped in his right hand. Stooping down, he caught a blazing brand with his left, swung it rapidly over his head a few times to give it additional blaze, and then darted away like a meteor directly among the wolverines. The latter scattered in greater terror than ever, but the Indian, instead of returning, actually followed them.

The brand could only be seen flitting among the trees, its flaming glare giving a wild, unearthly appearance to the face and breast of the Savage as he sped swiftly in and out among the trunks and vegetation, like an avenger bent on destroying the entire band.

One of the largest wolverines, in his wild fear, sprung so close to Elwood that his tail whisked against him. Ere he could clear himself the Indian burst upon him, his iron arm flashed out with lightning-like swiftness, the wire-like fingers caught the brute by the neck, and the knife was buried so deep in his throat that when he was thrown back he fell limp and dead to the ground. After which Shasta sat down upon the ground again, folded his blanket over his shoulders and appeared much occupied in contemplating the burning sticks before him.

"Mr. Shasta, that was well done!" exclaimed Tim in admiration. "I very much doubt whether it could be excelled by your humble servant, the undersigned."

"I very much doubt it also," said Elwood. "I shouldn't fancy chasing those animals with a firebrand."

"No; if you should drop it or fall down unpleasant cones-quences might follow."

The boys kept up their loading and firing among the wolverines until they had slain over a dozen. But instead of diminishing, the number continued to increase till there must have been nearly two-score growling, snapping and snarling around the camp-fire.

# CHAPTER XXXI

## SHASTA'S HUMOR

The camp-fire was kept burning unremittingly until morning, and the wolverines as unceasingly continued their clamor, so that none of the parties secured a moment's sleep. The boys were signaled several times by Shasta to lie down, but they were too unaccustomed to such sights and sounds to permit them to do so with anything like peace; so they used their rifles upon the savage animals until prudence advised them to husband their ammunition until they had better use for it.

Tim O'Rooney was fully as restless as they. He was in continual dread that some of the treacherous animals would steal up behind him and fasten their teeth so securely in him that they could not be shaken off. This uneasiness caused him ever to be shifting his position, now on one side the fire, now on the other—springing suddenly upward as though he already felt the nip of their fangs.

The Pah Utah, at this time, displayed a grim humor, so exceptional with his people, as to be almost incredible, except to the boys who were witnesses to it. Believing such traits should be encouraged among all aborigines as an antidote for their melancholy dispositions, it gives us great pleasure to record it, and it will afford us far greater enjoyment to testify regarding any other such performances that may come under our notice.

Tim was standing with his back toward the fire, and his hands, carelessly crossed behind him. He was intently watching the quarrelsome animals, and all thoughts of attack in the rear had for the time departed. Shasta leaned silently forward and lifted a small brand to relight his pipe, which had gone out some time before. As he was passing it back to the embers the red coal just grazed one of Tim's fingers, while at the same instant the Indian imitated the snarl of the wolverine so exactly that the follow was sure he was seized, and he made the most agile leap of his life.

"Murther! murther! pull him off, Mr. Shasta, catch hold of him!" exclaimed the affrighted Irishman, springing wildly on every side of the fire, and striking with blind fierceness at the imaginary brute in his rear.

Howard and Elwood laughed till the tears rolled down their cheeks. They had seen Shasta's trick and they could therefore appreciate it. Never a smile lit up the grim face of the Pah Utah. He continued leisurely smoking, his keen black eyes looking dreamily into the fire, as if lost in some pleasant reverie.

But what of that? Who can doubt, that he laughed internally full as heartily as the youngsters? Who can tell what surges, and waves, and ripples of laughter went through and through him, until his whole being was absorbed in merriment?

Finally Tim's terror passed away and he became comparatively quiet.

"Worrah! worrah!" he exclaimed, panting from his severe exertions. "What a narra 'scape I had."

"Did he really bite you?"

"Bite me! Didn't ye see him fasten his teeth in me and hang on till I shuk him off?"

"No; I didn't observe him."

"Git out wid ye nonsense. But I felt him sure and it was meself that thought once he'd pull me off into the darkness and make me a prey to the beasts there—that I did think, did I."

"No danger," remarked Howard, as he and his cousin were unable to restrain their laughter.

"What be ye spalpeens laughing at?" indignantly demanded the Irishman.

"But, Tim, are you sure you were not mistaken? We saw nothing of the kind," pursued Howard.

The fellow looked too full of indignation to speak.

"What is getting into your heads? Ye saam to be losing your sinses intirely."

"And I can say I saw none of them touch you."

"Then you was blind," was the indignant retort. "Ye harrd him sing out at me heels, didn't you?"

"Of course, we heard them all the time, as we do now; but the one you imagined so close may have been a dozen feet distant."

"*But he bit me!*" was the triumphant reply to this.

"Where?"

"On the hand."

"Let us see the mark!"

The boys arose and walked up to their friend, who bent over the fire, held his hand close to his face, turning it over and over and scrutinizing it with the closest attention. Concluding he was mistaken, he exchanged it for its fellow, which was subjected to an equally severe cross-examination. Still nothing confirmatory of his words could be found.

The amazed Irishman now held up both his hands, turning them over and over and pressing them close to his face.

"Do yees saa anything?" he abruptly asked, thrusting them toward the boys.

They went through the form of a search for a scratch or a bite, but declared themselves unable to discover any.

"Don't you feel any pain?" asked Howard.

"I thought I did," replied Tim, with a serious, puzzled look upon his countenance.

"In what part of your body?"

"Whisht!"

He motioned to them to maintain silence, while he closed his eyes and waited for some evidence of the pain he had so sharply felt a few minutes before. As he stood thus, he stealthily brought each hand around in front of his face and subjected them to the same examination.

Suddenly his eye sparkled, and he held out his left:

"That's the hand!" he exclaimed exultingly.

"Let's see?" asked the boys, stepping up to him.

"Yees'll find it somewhere there, if yees'll take the throuble to examine it closely."

They did so, but declared themselves unable to find the wound.

Tim finally showed a small red spot upon one of the fingers, which he affirmed was where the cruel tooth did bite him.

"That cannot be, for the skin is not broken."

"But it faals as if the same had been bit off."

"It looks more like a burn," added Elwood.

Tim now turned around and looked at the Pah Utah. The latter was smoking his pipe, as if unconscious of the presence of any being or animal near him. Perhaps they were mistaken, but Howard and Elwood always affirmed that they detected a twitching at the corners of his mouth, as if he were ready to explode with laughter.

But if it was that, it was nothing more, and it manifested itself in no other manner. Tim gazed fixedly at him a moment, and then turning to the boys, asked in a whisper:

*"But didn't ye hear it snarrl at meself?"*

# CHAPTER XXXII

## AGAIN ON THE RIVER

The Newfoundland, Terror, occasioned more apprehension to his friends than did anything else. They came to see that no personal danger threatened so long as the fire kept burning, and as there was an abundance of fuel, this settled that point; but the dog grew enraged at the furious uproar, which drove away all sleep, and appeared to give him fear that the entire party were in danger.

Several times, when some of the wolverines came too close, he made a spring at them, and they snapped back. But the good sense of the dog kept him from venturing among the ravenous brutes, and they in turn were in too much dread of the fire to do more than spring at him and then as quickly dart back again.

It was an impressive sight and one which could never be forgotten. The large, noble Newfoundland, standing out in relief against the glare of the camp-fire, his eyes aflame with anger, every muscle braced, the jaws parted and his eyes fixed upon the dark bodies plunging over each other, darting forward and back again, snapping, snarling and furious; the Pah Utah stretched upon the ground, deliberately smoking, all unheedful of the deafening clangor and the savage brutes

Edward S. Ellis

that sometimes approached almost within striking distance; the two boys, so close to the fire that they were often scorched by it, gazing at the animals with an expression of half fear and half wonder, starting when one of them came unusually near, and now and then sending the fatal bullet among them; the nervous Irishman, darting hither and thither, taking great care that the fire was kept fully burning; all these, we say, made a scene impressive in the highest degree.

Terror, when sharply spoken to, would withdraw from his dangerous proximity to the wolverines, but almost immediately he stepped forward to the same spot he first occupied, and his obedience to the commands of the boys was so sullen and ill-natured that they forebore speaking to him except when his safety seemed absolutely to demand it.

At times there was an interruption in the clamor, but the wolverines did not appear to relax their vigilance in the least. It was as if they had determined to make their evening meal upon the party though they were forced to wait until morning for it. During these intervals of comparative silence our friends gained opportunity for the exchange of a few words, but they were often compelled to shout at the top of their voices to make themselves heard.

During one of these lulls Elwood spoke to Howard.

"What will take place in the morning, when these creatures are not afraid of our fire?"

"I think they will go away."

"Perhaps so: but we are not so sure of that."

"Shasta will no doubt turn the whole thing over in his mind, and be prompt enough to act when the danger comes. I suppose we can take to our canoes and give them the slip in that manner."

"Yes; the Indian appears to have rather a contemptible opinion of them. He scarcely heeds their wrangling."

"He is not so timid as we and Tim are; but he doesn't forget to look at them once in a while, so as not to forget what they are doing."

"They are a savage set of animals. How angry Terror is! Don't you notice that they are trying to entice him to venture out a little nearer them? They hate him more than all of us."

"Do you think so?"

"You can see it in their manner. If they can once get hold of him they will tear him to shreds."

"And they will catch him, too, if he isn't careful. He is so surly and cross himself that it is dangerous to touch or speak to him."

"We can't afford to lose him. We must watch, and if he gets too close to any of them, why, all we shall have to do is to crack them over, and give the others warning to keep their distance."

While they were speaking a huge wolverine darted close enough to strike Terror. Instantly the two closed and rolled upon the ground in the fierce death struggle. Over and over, snapping, snarling, growling, biting, scratching with lightning-like fierceness, now one below and then the other, and finally the dog on top.

The conflict was as short as it was furious. The massive jaws of the Newfoundland closed on the throat of his antagonist and his teeth met through his windpipe. There they stuck for a minute, and when he relaxed his hold it was all over with the reckless animal.

Still it would have fared ill with the dog but for Shasta, for the other wolverines would have sprung upon him and destroyed him before he could have escaped. At the moment the two closed the Indian darted forward, seized a brand and flourished it over the combatants. This so terrified the others that they kept their distance until the conqueror resumed his place in triumph by the fire.

This encounter proved it lesson to both the dog and the wolverines. The latter appeared to comprehend the disadvantage under which they were placed, while Terror, having had a taste of their mettle, was satisfied for the time, and kept a safe position further away from the brutes that were so eager to fasten their teeth in him.

It was now verging toward morning, and the Pah Utah looked about him as if he were going to make his preparations for moving. He looked toward the raging creatures, still fierce and furious, and then glanced at the canoes drawn up within a few feet of the camp-fire, and pointed toward them and the river.

Fortunately but a few feet intervened between their present position and the stream, so that the latter was easy of access in case it should become necessary to retreat before the wolverines. Still the fire did not protect this enough to make it a safe undertaking in their present situation.

Shasta picked up several blazing sticks, and carrying them to the water's edge, placed them together and covered them with some dry brush-wood. They speedily fanned themselves into a flame, and the gathering brutes withdrew and offered a fine approach to the river.

The Indian's next proceeding was to launch the two boats. This was done easily and without difficulty. The blankets and guns were placed within, and then motioned for the dog to follow; but Terror did not seem disposed to leave his present quarters. Perhaps the idea worked its way into his shaggy head that it savored too much of deserting his friends, or it may be that he still coveted a taste for another collision with the audacious animals that had pressed him so sorely.

Our brave soldier boys, who abhor bloodshed from a principle, still have a love for the wild abandon of camp life, and many a one looks back with a sigh to the rough experiences which we all pray may never come again. So it may be the Newfoundland, naturally peaceful, having had his blood fairly roused by his tussle and triumph, yet longed for more of victory.

Finally Howard and Elwood took their seats, and Tim O'Rooney followed; then Terror, casting one reluctant look behind him, jumped into the boat and lay down in his usual position; and so, at length, they all were embarked in safety.

Edward S. Ellis

# CHAPTER XXXIII

## A HALT

It was just growing light as the two canoes shoved out in the river and resumed their journey. The rapacious wolverines, enraged at the loss of their expected prey, followed them to the very edge of the stream, where their ear-splitting clamor grew more furious than ever. At one time, indeed, it looked us though they were about to jump into the water and swim out to them; and both the boys looked inquiringly at the face of the Pah Utah. The stolid, indifferent expression that they there saw relieved them, and they withdrew all further thought regarding the troublesome animals.

Shasta had loosened the connection between the two boats—not, perhaps, that he was unwilling to carry them also along, but because he judged it was time that the party learned to navigate for themselves.

Tim O'Rooney grasped the paddle, and his handling of it showed no ordinary skill. He had greatly improved upon his performance of yesterday, and kept his position slightly in the rear of the other canoe, whose owner, as a matter of course, timed his speed to that of his pupil.

When the Irishman was tired he passed the paddle to

Howard, who had been carefully studying the "style" of Shasta, and whose efforts were modeled after his. Practice alone can make perfect, no matter if the theory in absolutely so. The mind may hold the exact idea, and may send the precise message through the nerves to the muscles, but the latter must make a good many trials before they can carry out orders with exactness.

And so the boy, although, as he believed, he imitated exactly the manner of their dusky friend, was not long in finding that the paddle was by no means as obedient. The reason was that the delicate play of the iron muscles of the Pah Utah could not be seen. They had done this thing so often that it became a matter of course with them.

But having started upon right principles, by the time the boy was so exhausted that he could not move his arms, he could see that he had improved, or as the sovereign people say, "he was getting the knack of it." It was now Elwood's turn, and he caught the paddle with all the enthusiasm which might be expected in a youngster who had been impatiently waiting to take part in some game.

By the time Elwood needed rest, Tim O'Rooney was ready, and so the paddle did unceasing work, each member having all the time necessary for rest, until after they had been to work some hours, the boys found their arms remained tired, and a longer cessation needed.

Shasta seemed to look upon these essays of his friends with no little pleasure. He watched their movements all the time, and a horrible suspicion once entered the head of Tim O'Rooney that he saw him come very near smiling. Whether there were any grounds for this suspicion probably will never be known, unless the Pah Utah takes it into his head to write and tell us.

Edward S. Ellis

Shasta remained a few feet in advance, his back being placed toward the prow of his own boat. This relative position—and our "pale faced" friends, it may be said, labored savagely—was kept by him without any effort. Now and then he touched the point of his paddle, but there was scarcely a ripple. It was as a fish is sometimes seen to move through the water with the slightest quiver of its fins.

When all three of our friends were used up, red in the face, panting and sighing for a chance to take a good long rest, a tiny island came in view round a bend in the river, and to their joy they saw Shasta fix his eye upon it and then head his canoe toward the point. Cheered by the prospect, they renewed their work with greater ardor, and in a few moments the boats buried their points in the luxuriant undergrowth along the shore.

The island was quite small, and offered no inducements in the way of game, unless some animal in crossing the river had paused to rest itself and make an exploration of the place. This was scarcely to be expected, and none of the party based any hopes upon it.

After the inmates of the large canoe had stepped upon shore, Shasta sent his backward into the river again by a sweep of his paddle, and headed for the eastern bank, shooting over the surface with amazing speed. His movements were watched with interest and some surprise.

"What can it mean?" asked Elwood.

"Perhaps he is going to leave us."

"I don't think he would do it in that manner. He will make an elaborate good-by for us, for we are getting to understand each other quite well by means of signs."

"Arrah now!" exclaimed Tim O'Rooney, "didn't ye saa that he was disgusted wid our paddling and kaaping him back, and has gone out jist that he may enj'y the pleasure of shtretching his arms in the owld-fashioned manner, as Father O'Shaughnessy said when he tipped over his brother?"

This may have satisfied the Irishman, but hardly the boys. It did not look reasonable to them that the Indian, having just finished three times the amount of work performed by each, was in so great need of additional exercise that he must abandon his friends and paddle off over the river.

"I think he is going to hunt for fish," said Elwood.

"But he could have caught them without going to land."

"Perhaps not. I noticed yesterday that he went where there was a sort of eddy, and you see he can't find that very well unless it is close by land."

Howard pointed to the lower end of the island:

"What better place could he find than that? It is just the spot to catch fish."

By this time Shasta's canoe had reached the bank, but instead of landing he turned the prow down stream, and slowly glided along as if in quest of something. This to Tim O'Rooney was proof of the truth of his declaration.

"What did I tell yees? The thrip to shore was not enough, and he's taking a wee turn further."

"He is looking for a good fishing ground," affirmed Howard. "If it were anything else he would not go so slowly."

"But, see! he has stopped?"

As Elwood spoke the Pah Utah rose in his canoe and stepped ashore. He stooped and employed himself a moment with the canoe and then disappeared.

"It cannot be that he has left us," said Elwood, in considerable alarm.

"No; I think he is hunting for game."

This seemed very reasonable, and the party waited patiently for his return. No personal danger to himself could be expected, as he could not be approached undiscovered by any hostile white man, and being an Indian he could have no cause to fear anything from his own race.

Still there was a vague misgiving that everything was not right—that something unusual would be the result of this separation—and each member of the little party awaited, with more anxiety than he would have confessed, some evidence of the intention of the Pah Utah.

# CHAPTER XXXIV

## EXIT SHASTA

The three whites were still gazing toward the eastern shore, intently looking for some sign, or listening to some sound which might tell something regarding Shasta, when they were startled by a loud whirring or buzzing overhead, and looking up saw a large bird passing within a few feet of them—so close that its claws could be seen curled up against its body, as it made a sudden sweep to the right, frightened at its near approach to its human enemies.

"Shoot it!" called out Elwood to Howard. "My gun isn't loaded, and it will make us a good breakfast."

But the bird, whatever it was, did not choose to wait until the heavy rifle could be brought to bear upon it; and by the time Howard had fairly got the idea through his head, it was skimming away over the country toward the Coast Range.

But a sharper eye and an unerring aim was leveled against it, and as they were watching its flight it suddenly turned over and over, its great wings going like the arms of a windmill as it dropped swiftly to the earth; and, as it disappeared in the trees and undergrowth, the crack of a rifle came across the intervening space.

"That was Shasta!" exclaimed Elwood in delight.

"Certainly, we might have known what he was after. He thinks we do not admire fish as a steady diet and has gone after fowl for us."

"I don't know about that," said Elwood, who sometimes seemed to alternate with Howard in his knowledge of the ways of the wood. "I can't see that there was any more chance of seeing birds there than upon the island. That same fowl passed closer to us than it did to him."

"I suppose," laughed Howard, "that he was hunting after game of some kind, and had no idea of shooting the bird until it passed so near him that he saw it was quite the thing we needed, and so he toppled it over."

"Me views intirely," assented Tim. "I agraas wid both of yees."

A few moments later the Pah Utah appeared with the bird in his hand, and flinging it into the canoe quickly paddled back to the island. His bird proved to be a species of wild goose, that seemed to have strayed from its flock and gone wandering through the Salinas Valley at this season of the year ultimately to fall before the rifle of Shasta.

Our friends were in ecstasies over their prospective meal. The Indian displayed the same skill in dressing the bird that he did in preparing the fish. The feathers were quickly twitched off, and the dry driftwood piled upon the upper end of the island was the best fuel they could have had for the purpose. When done, it was "done brown," and to a turn; and to the famishing travelers nothing could have been more savory and luscious.

The truth of it was, the boys found that this kind of life was agreeing with them amazingly. Their appetites were fierce, their sleep sound, and a feeling of perfect health diffused itself through their glowing frames, such as they had never known before. Their exposure to the night air troubled them at first, but they soon recovered from it and enjoyed "camping out" as thoroughly as did old campaigners.

It was a very good thing, it is true, for a while; but don't let any boys get the idea of following their example, unless they are compelled in precisely the same manner to do so. If any youngster imagines he has formed true ideas of distant countries from the narratives of adventures which he may have read, he will find himself most woefully mistaken. Never think of traveling until you are a married man, and by that time you will have made up your mind to be sensible and stay at home.

When the meal was finished, and their appetites satisfied, the Pah Utah, instead of immediately embarking, walked to the lower end of the island, and stood for some time apparently examining some sign further down the river. Following the direction of his eyes, our friends could see nothing unusual until Elwood detected something in the air on the western bank which at first resembled a light cloud, but which they imagined might be caused by a camp-fire.

Whatever it was that attracted the attention of Shasta he took but a few moments to decide regarding it. Going again to his canoe, he entered it without a word or sign, and paddled away at his swiftest rate straight toward it, while his companions watched the proceeding with as much interest as in the preceding case.

The camp appeared fully a half-mile distant, and it took but a short time for the Indian to reach a point opposite, when he

Edward S. Ellis

sprung lightly ashore and disappeared with his usual celerity.

"He is cautious," remarked Elwood. "He doesn't wish us to undertake to pass it unless he is sure there will be no trouble."

"A sinsible young man!" asserted Tim. "His parents have the best raison for faaling proud of so promising a young gintleman."

"And so have we."

A few moments elapsed, when the Pah Utah reappeared and came back as rapidly as he went.

The first thing he did upon reaching the island was again to fasten the boats together, and then motion to the three to enter. This, of course, they did without delay, and took their usual positions.

But Shasta was not satisfied. He told them, in his manner, to lie down; and not until the three had so arranged themselves as to be invisible from both shores, did he dip his paddle and resume his journey.

"This means danger," said Elwood. "He doesn't wish any one to know we are in the boats."

"And we must be sure and obey him."

"It's aisy doing, as my brother used to say whin his wife tould him, in her gintle manner, by the help of her broomstick, to go to bed."

"And, Elwood, you are close to Terror, see that he doesn't let his curiosity got the better of his judgment."

The Pah Utah was satisfied, and now began plying his paddle. It was difficult for the three so to govern their curiosity as not to peep over the side of the canoe; but there were good reasons for their not doing so, and they scarcely moved a limb for the next hour.

They had gone but a little way when Terror raised his head and uttered a slight bark; but a word from Elwood quieted him. Finally, Shasta paused and uttered a guttural sound in his own tongue, which was taken as permission for them to rise.

As they did so, they looked behind. The dim smoke ascending in the summer sky was seen far behind, and between it and them the Salinas made another bend, so that they had no cause to fear observation from that party at least.

Shasta again disconnected the two canoes—an act which did not surprise them; but his next proceeding astonished them a good deal.

Reaching across the boats, he shook hands with them all, at the same time muttering a word or two to each.

"He is going to leave us," said Elwood, with an air of disappointment.

"He has good reason for doing so, but I am afraid it will be bad for us."

"Adieu, Mr. Shasta, adieu!" said Tim O'Rooney, with considerable feeling. "You've done us a good turn and we'll not forget you. If yez ever drifts into San Francisco, give us a call."

The Indian motioned to them to proceed, and using his paddle with his extraordinary skill, he sped up the river toward the camp-fire, and in a very short time vanished.

Edward S. Ellis

# CHAPTER XXXV

## THE WESTERN SHORE

The departure of Shasta gave rise to all manner of doubt and speculation. None of them believed he meditated bidding the party good-by until he went through the ceremony of shaking hands. This settled the matter, and they could have no cause for hope of seeing him again.

"That must have been a party of his people," said Howard, "or he would not have taken the pains to help us out of sight."

"At any rate, he has done us good service," replied Elwood. "I don't know what would have become of us but for him."

They had not yet begun using their paddle, but were drifting with the current, debating upon their course of action.

"I think I understand why he left us," added Howard, after a moment's pause.

Tim and Elwood looked up in his face.

"I think we have passed through most of the danger, and he thought we were just as safe without him as with him. Don't you see, Elwood, that we have come a good ways down the river, and we must be near some settlement. I think there is a place called Soledad somewhere along this river, but whether on the eastern or western bank I cannot tell."

"It is a good ways off, I should say fifty miles, and is on the western bank."

"How comes it that *you* are so well informed?" asked Howard, repeating the question that had been asked him by his cousin when on the steamer.

"It is only accidentally that I know that. A few weeks ago I was comparing an old and new geography and noticed what different views they gave of the western part of our country. The old maps had the Buenaventura so wrong in every particular that I learned considerable about the true one, which you know is called Salinas by most people."

"If we are very careful, I think we can get home without trouble; but although there must be white people—settlers and miners—in these parts, still they are so scattered that we are less likely to see them than we are the Indians."

"Boys," said Tim O'Rooney, who had not let his pipe go out since morning. "Shall I give yez some good advice?"

Both expressed their eagerness to receive it.

"There bees plenty of the rid gintlemen yet in this counthry, and we haven't got beyant them. If we goes paddling in this canoe when the sun is shining overhead, some of 'em will see us, and if we don't put into shore they'll put out after us—that they will."

"What is it that you propose, then?"

"That we turns the night into day, and slaaps and smokes and meditates by sunlight, and does our traveling by moonlight, or what is bether, without any light at all."

This proposal suited the boys exactly. It was so plainly dictated by common sense that the wonder was they had not thought of it long before. Elwood took the paddle in his hand and held it poised.

"Which way—east or west?"

Howard pointed to the left bank.

"That is the side where *they* are," replied Elwood, referring to the Indian party they had passed.

"And where *he* is," meaning their good friend, the Pah Utah.

"To the left—to the left," said Tim. "Didn't I git into the worst throuble of me life—always barring the repulse me Bridget give me—by hunting in them parts?"

Elwood delayed no longer, but plied the oars with a dexterity that showed his experience had not been lost upon him.

"You understand it quite well," said Howard approvingly.

"Yes; but my arms ache terribly."

"Ah! here we are."

The prow of the canoe moved as silently and easily into the undergrowth as if it were water, and our friends at a step passed from every portion of it to dry land.

As they intended remaining in their present quarters until

darkness, they took some pains to select a suitable place. They finally hit upon a spot, on an incline of the river bank, and about a dozen yards distant. Here the grass was green and velvety, and the wood so thick that they had little fear of discovery, unless by some who had seen them land and took the trouble to hunt them out.

It was about noon when they landed, and as they had all spent a wakeful night, their first proceeding was so to arrange themselves as to enjoy a quiet sleep. Terror was placed on duty as sentinel, and all lay down with a sense of security to which they had been strangers in a long time.

As usual, the boys were the first to awake, doing so almost at the same moment. They saw by the sun that the afternoon was about half gone, but they were not troubled from hunger, as their morning meal may be said to have been their midday one, and had been one of those royal ones whose memory is apt to linger a long time with us, especially if we are boys.

"This is tiresome," said Elwood, yawning and stretching his limbs, "let us take a tramp of discovery."

The proposal suited Howard, although prudence told him to remain where he was and keep his friend with him. But the restraint was so irksome that he was all too willing a listener to the persuasions of his companion.

"I noticed there was quite a high range of hills just back of us," added Elwood. "Let's take a look at them."

"Is it prudent?" and Howard only repeated audibly the question that his conscience had just asked him.

"Prudent? Of course it is, if we only take good care of ourselves."

"Shall we awake Tim before we go?"

"No; he will sleep until to-morrow morning."

"We must leave Terror to watch him then, for it wouldn't do for him to lie alone and asleep."

"Of course not."

The Newfoundland, which had risen to his feet, was told to remain on guard, and the boys started off on a ramble that was to be a most eventful one to them.

# CHAPTER XXXVI

## THE RAMBLE

After the restraint the boys had undergone, cramped in the canoe, and not daring to wander out of sight of their campfire when upon shore, there was a delicious relief in rambling through the woods. The clear, pure air that was dry and cool in the shadow of the forest, the undulating, charming scenery, the novel look that rested upon all they saw—these possessed a charm to our young friends which they hardly could have resisted, even if they had the will to do so; but when we say that after starting forth scarcely a thought of their imprudence entered their heads, it was but natural that they should find themselves led much further away than was either wise or consistent with the resolves with which they left their friends, Tim and Terror.

They took no notice of the direction they were following, nor of the distance they had gone, until near the middle of the afternoon Howard abruptly paused and asked, with a look of alarm:

"Elwood, what have we done?"

"Why? What is the matter?"

"We must be a mile off from Tim, and it will be dark before we can get back."

"O! I think not. You know we have walked very slowly, and we can hurry when we take it into our heads to return."

"But do you know the way?"

"Certainly. Don't you?"

"What course must we follow?"

Elwood pointed to the northwest, which, while it was not far from their general course, was by no means the proper one by which to rejoin their companion.

"How strange!" said Howard. "It seems to me that yonder is the point from which we started."

And *he* pointed nearly due west, just as wrong as he could possibly be.

"You are wrong," said Elwood positively. "I am sure of the right way."

"We won't dispute over it," replied his companion, with some sadness, "for it is very doubtful if either of us is right."

"All we have to do then, is to hunt for the river and follow that up until we find Tim sound asleep."

"Yea; but how is the river to be found? To you it lies in one place, and to me in another."

"But I can prove that you are wrong, and," laughed Elwood, "that I am, too, although I was never right."

"How so?"

"The sun sets in the west, and notice where it is."

Howard now opened his eyes in amazement. He would have been sure that it was going down in the other part of the sky; but the proof before his eyes was irrefragable.

"It must be," he replied. "We have been 'turned round.' Just as when we left the wharf at New York. I was below when the steamer came out, and so long as New York was in sight I was sure it lay in the wrong place."

"But, how bad even that makes it! We cannot reach the river before dark, and we shall not know whether we am a mile above or below where Tim is sleeping."

"If we go straight for the river, I think it likely that we shall come much nearer him than that."

"It may be, but how are we to tell?"

"Why, if we don't find him by night, we can fire oft our guns and call to him."

"And bring a party of the savages down upon us."

"That may be if there are any in the neighborhood, but we shall have to run the risk."

By this time the boys were fully impressed with their want of discretion and with the urgent necessity of making all haste back to the river.

"Let us keep our thoughts about us," said Howard, "for we have been without them long enough. Now, the Salinas River runs very nearly north and south, doesn't it?"

"This portion of it does."

"Then we must go as nearly east as we can, and let's be off."

Turning their backs upon the sun, they began retracing their steps; but they had journeyed scarce half an hour when they found themselves near a range of hills, which they were sure they had not passed through, and did not remember to have seen.

"What does this mean?" asked Howard, still more alarmed. "We never have been near these."

"Are they not the hills we noticed just us we were about starting?"

"They cannot be;—these are larger, have not half as much wood upon them. I tell you, Elwood, there is one thing sure."

"I know what you mean."

"What is it?"

*"We are lost!"*

"You are right. We may find Tim again, but we are going to have trouble to do it."

"Listen! He may call to us."

They stopped walking find held their breath, but not a sound broke the solemn stillness, save a faint, hollow roar— whether the deep murmur that is always heard in a great forest, or the sound of the distant Pacific Ocean they could not tell.

"No; he is asleep yet," said Elwood. "If he would only wake up he would shout to us."

"Thus you see, if we shoot our guns, the chances are that *he* will not hear it, while it may be the means of bringing to us the very ones we are so anxious to keep away."

So they concluded not to fire their rifles for the present.

"But these hills," continued Howard, "they don't extend in any great direction either north or south. The question now is, shall we pass around the northern or southern end?"

"What difference will it make?"

"All the difference in the world. If Tim is to the south of us, and we pass around that way, I think we shall find him without much hunting, while if we take the wrong course it will be night before we can get anywhere near him."

"I see," replied Elwood. "We shall have to guess at it. But, hold!" he exclaimed, with sparkling eyes. "You go one way and I will another!"

Howard shook his head.

"There is too much risk."

"Not at all. The distance is short, and we can whistle to each other every few minutes. Then, you know, as we shall be looking for each other, we cannot lose ourselves in these still woods. The minute I get sight of the river I can tell whether we are above or below Tim."

Edward S. Ellis

Howard would not consent at first, but his cousin set forth the advantages of the plan so eloquently that he finally agreed. Arranging their signals and manner of proceeding, the boys, therefore, separated.

# CHAPTER XXXVII

## BACK TO CAMP

The hill which the boys proposed to pass around was about a quarter of a mile in length and but slightly less in breadth—much greater than either of them suspected when they set out. It rose like a peak to the height of several hundred feet, as if it were an offshoot from the main ridge of hills, left to flourish by itself.

Howard walked slowly along, after glancing back at his cousin until the intervening wood concealed him from view, when he gave a short, sharp whistle, which was immediately answered. Then, appreciating the necessity of haste, he quickened his footsteps.

As he advanced the hills assumed proportions of which he had not dreamed, and that raised in his mind strong doubts as to the wisdom of separating from his companion. He would not have done it had not the latter urged him so. Misgivings now arose in the mind of the boy. He looked upon his duty as that of restraining and tempering Elwood's impulsiveness. He had done so several times to his manifest advantage; but on this day, as Howard looked back, it really appeared as if he had bidden good-by to his senses. Their separation from Tim was almost criminal in its foolishness, and yet he had scarcely raised an objection; and now, was not the last proceeding still more imprudent? As it stood, the three members of the little party who should never have been out of each other's sight, were now a good distance from each other, and that, too, when in a hostile country.

From these rather sad reflections Howard was roused by the faint, echoing whistle of Elwood.

"He is all right," thought he, feeling much relieved, as he placed his fingers to his mouth and returned the whistle. "We are both now passing around the hill, so that we cannot get further apart, and can keep within call all the time."

Admonished by the lateness of the hour, Howard almost ran. He grew somewhat impatient at the unexpected extent of the hill; but finally he passed beyond the southern point, and as he stood and listened, he heard the murmur of the river— proof that it was close at hand.

"Now," thought he, "if Elwood will only hurry, we have a good chance of finding Tim before he gives us up for lost."

The boy could not see that anything at all was gained by their course in passing around the ridge. Neither of them, were in sight of the river, and would have to advance still further before they could form any idea of their whereabouts. He was resolved to do this in company with his cousin, so that precisely the same thing would have been accomplished had they remained together.

Howard having hurried a great deal, thought it likely that he was some distance in advance of his cousin. He stood some minutes listening for his signals, and then began walking toward the northern end of the hill that he might meet him as he came around. He observed as he advanced that they increased in rocky ruggedness, and could see that it was quite a feat to pass through them.

Going some distance he paused again, and listened intently, but nothing beside the deep murmur of the woods reached his ear.

"What can it mean?" he finally asked himself, as a vague alarm crept over him. "We must be much closer together than we were before, and I haven't heard him whistle for the last half-hour."

He began to doubt whether it was best to proceed further or not. It might serve only to mislead in case Elwood was searching for him. Still hearing nothing to indicate the location of his friend, he made the signal himself—a long, screeching whistle, that rang out in the solemn stillness with a penetrating clearness that sent the chills over him from head to foot.

"He must hear that if he is within a mile," was his reflection, as he leaned his head forward and listened for the first approach of the answering sound.

Ten, fifteen, twenty minutes passed away, but nothing was heard, and the poor boy looked around in sore alarm.

"Can it be that Elwood is jesting?" he asked himself. "He would not do so if he knew what I am suffering."

Howard was now in great distress. He could not decide what to do. If he advanced he could feel no assurance of meeting his friend, while a retreat was equally hopeless.

Where was Elwood? Had he wandered off among the hills, tempted by the wild scenery, and had he lost his way? Was he searching for his cousin? Or had he been found by Indians?

The last inquiry had been rising in Howard's mind for a half-hour, but he had resolutely forced it down again, until he could keep it away no longer. He could find no other reason to account for the silence, and failure to answer his call. The whistle which he had given must have spread miles in every direction—so far that Elwood could not have got beyond its range had the course of both been precisely opposite. No; it must—

But, hark! A faint, tremulous whistle comes to his ear. It is far away and sounds among the hills behind, as though it had labored up from some cave or chasm miles distant. Howard held his breath, and as he anticipated, it came again so faintly and distantly that had he been walking he could not have heard it.

On both occasions it sounded behind him among the hills, though its tremulous faintness made it appear as though it came from far up in the air, or down deep in some of the gorges of the hills—so uncertain was the exact point of its starting.

Poor Howard was now in a dilemma. Whether to attempt to follow up the signal or to go on to the river and search out Tim O'Rooney and the Newfoundland was a question which was difficult to decide. But his eagerness to find his cousin led him on into the hills, until he had penetrated quite a distance. He then paused and listened for the signal, but none was ever to come to his ears again.

Howard repeated the whistle over and over, and finally fired his gun; but both were equally fruitless. He waited where he was until dark, when with a sad heart he withdrew and resumed his tramp toward the river. Gloomy indeed were his meditations, as he reflected on the occurrences of the day, and there was scarcely anything he would not do, if by any means he could recall *his* part since he landed upon the main shore.

In the course of half an hour he reached the river, and looked intently out into the semi-darkness to see whether he could recognize anything familiar; but so far as he was able to see, all was strange, from which he concluded that he had struck at a point lower down than where Tim had been left.

He therefore began making his way south, that is, toward the source of the river, after halting and listening for some sound that might tell something either of Tim or Elwood. Suddenly a threatening growl startled him, and then came the welcome bark of Terror, and the next moment the dog was frolicking around him and showing his delight in the most extravagant manner.

# CHAPTER XXXVIII

## WAITING AND WATCHING

"Worrah! worrah! but this is a fine scare you've been givin' Tim O'Rooney, so me uncle said whin they towld him his wife was coming over to Ameriky to see him. Here I've been awake fur the last two hours, jist, looking and expacting you to come back, and thinking the red colored gintleman had carried you away entirely—"

Howard impatiently interrupted him.

"Have you seen or heard anything of Elwood?"

"No-o-o!" replied Tim, his answer rising and falling in a circumflex through a half-dozen notes of the scale.

*"Then he is lost!"*

"What?" fairly shrieked the Irishman.

"He is lost in the woods."

Howard had little heart to go over the experiences of the afternoon. He simply told his friend that he and Elwood had separated on their return, and he had been unable to find him again.

"What did you separate for?" asked the listener.

"Because I was a fool; but O, Tim, there is no use of regretting what has been done. If Elwood is lost, I shall never leave this place."

After a while Howard became more composed, and they conversed rationally upon the best plan for them to follow. Tim O'Rooney was strenuous in his belief that Elwood had wandered off among the hills, and finding it growing dark, had sought some secure shelter for the night. He was sure that he would give vigorous signs of his whereabouts as soon as day dawned.

There was something in the daring nature of the boy that made it probable that Tim was right. Tempted out of his path by some singular or unexpected sight, he had wandered away until he found it too dark to return, and so had made the best of the matter and camped in some tree, or beneath the ledge of some projecting rock.

Such was the theory of Tim O'Rooney, and so ingeniously did he enforce it that Howard could not avoid its plausibility. None knew better than he the impulsive nature of the boy, and such an act upon his part would be in perfect keeping with similar exploits.

There was but one thing that raised a doubt in the mind of Howard—and slight as was this, it was enough to give him sore uneasiness, and at times almost to destroy hope. At the time the boys separated, Elwood had shown a great anxiety to reach Tim, and proposed his plan in the belief that it would bring them together the more quickly.

Edward S. Ellis

This made it seem improbable to Howard that he would have allowed anything to divert him from his course unless his personal safety caused him to do so; but Tim said that if such were the case they would have heard his gun.

"Do you s'pose he's the boy to lit a wild animal or any of them red gintlemen step up to him without his tachin' thim manners? But he's the youngster that wouldn't do the same. You'd hear that gun of his cracking away as long as there was any lift for him to crack."

"It may be as you think, Tim, but I believe it is worse. Suppose he is in the hands of some of these wandering bands of Indians."

"S'pose he isn't."

"We have done that; but let us face the worst. If he has been taken away by them, what shall we do?"

"Hunt him up."

"That is true, but how that is to be done is the difficulty. If we only had Shasta with us."

"Arrah, now, if ye'd had him ye'd've niver gone thramping off in the woods and having me alone here with the dog. The red gintleman knowed what was best for us, and do ye mind, he kept his eye upon yez all the time."

Howard had thought the same thing a score of times since noon, and there was no need of his being told how the Pah Utah would have acted had he remained with them.

"I thinks Mr. Shasta isn't a great many miles off. P'rhaps," added Tim, significantly, "he's kapin' watch upon us and will come to our help in our throuble."

But the contingency, to Howard at least, was too remote for him to build any hopes upon it. It seemed more probable that the Indian's friendship had led him much further out of the way than they had suspected, and that he was now many a long mile off, speeding toward home.

"He may find out that the youngster is wid 'em," added Tim, "whin he will hasten to his relaaf."

"That seems the most likely."

"There's but one thing agin it."

"And what is that?"

But the Irishman was silent. The boy repeated his question.

"It's bad—let it be."

But Howard insisted.

"Wal, you know, they may—wal—*put him out the way.*"

"O Tim!" groaned Howard, "that cannot be, that cannot be!"

"I hopes not, but there's no telling what these sarpints may take into their heads to do. They're a bad set of craytures, always barring Mr. Shasta, and I'd've thought a good daal more of the same if he'd only staid a few days longer wid us."

"He thought we had enough sense to take care of ourselves, after he had seen us through the most dangerous part of our journey, otherwise he would have remained with us to the end. But, as I said a minute ago, it does no good for us to lament what cannot be helped. As soon as it is light we must go up among the hills with Terror and make a hunt for Elwood."

"Yees spake the truth. The dog may be smarter than we is, and I'm thinkin' it wouldn't have to be very smart to be in that same fix, and we'll sarch till we finds out something about him."

"It is fortunate for poor Elwood that the night is so mild and pleasant."

"Fort'nit for ourselves, be the same towken; for without our fire we'd be rather cool when we slept, and the cold would keep us awake all night."

"But we have the blanket with us, and that would protect us at any time, no matter how cold it might be."

"Yis," assented Tim, with a great sigh. "If I only had me pipe under way I'd faal somewhat more comfortable, barring the worriment I faals at the absence of the youngster. May God watch over him through the darkniss!"

"Amen!" was this reverent response of Howard.

# CHAPTER XXXIX

## THE SEARCH

All through the night Tim O'Rooney and Howard Lawrence sat in close consultation. Hunger and sleep were alike unthought of. Elwood Brandon was lost, and that was all of which they could think or speak. How they longed for the morning, and how impatient they were to be on the hunt! It seemed to Howard as if he could go leaping and flying down the chasms and gorges among the hills, and never tire until he had hunted out and brought back his cousin. Where could he be? If nestling in the branches of a tree, or hid away among the rocks, was he asleep? Or if awake, of what was he thinking? Did he believe that Howard was searching for him? Or did he imagine him also lost? It would not be reasonable to suppose that he had any suspicion of his finding Tim O'Rooney.

If in the hands of California Indians—But it would be vain to trace out all the thoughts and speculations that ran through the head of the boy. Some of them were of the wildest and most grotesque character, and would assume a ludicrous phase to one whose mind was not in such a whirl of excitement and distress.

In the gloom of the wood the darkness was so intense that

Edward S. Ellis

neither Tim nor Howard could distinguish each other, though only a few feet apart. The Newfoundland lay close to his master, seemingly sound asleep, but more heedful than the two of the approach of danger.

Occasionally through the night the call of some wild animal was heard—sometimes distant and sometimes so near that they started to their feet and were about to enter their canoe and shove out into the stream; but when it came no more they were reassured. Then something like the report of a gun came faintly up the river to their ears.

These sounds only served to render the night more gloomy and lonely, and to make the daylight the more welcome.

"Now let's be off," said Howard, as soon as it was light enough to distinguish each other's faces.

"We must find some means of remembering this place, or we'll never see the canoe agin, and will be obliged to sail into San Francisco on fut."

The boat was drawn entirely out of the water and covered as much as possible with leaves and undergrowth; for it was a loss that under any circumstances they could not sustain. The feat of marking the place so that they could readily return to it from any direction was more difficult; but Howard finally hit upon quite an ingenious scheme. They waited until the sun had approached near enough to the horizon that they could tell precisely the point where it would appear, and then turning their backs against it they walked forward until they reached the hills where Elwood had disappeared. Here they noticed the character and formation of the rocks so particularly that they could recognize them the moment they saw them. Thus the hills were such a conspicuous landmark as to be seen from a great distance; and, as they did not intend to go out of their sight, all they had to do was to hunt till they found this spot, and then walk due east.

All this was agreed upon, and they were among the hills just as the sun was coming up the horizon. Here, after whistling and shouting for sometime without receiving any response, they concluded to search for the point where the boys separated. This was quite distant, and over an hour was required to find the place, and when it was discovered Howard could not be positive that he was right.

But as time was of the greatest importance, they pressed on, the dog snuffing the ground as though he had scented the footprints, but he failed to follow them with certainty. Several hundred yards brought them to an opening in the hills just broad enough to admit the body of a man. It was not a tunnel-like opening, but a rent, as if the hills had been pulled a few feet asunder by the power of an earthquake.

The two paused in doubt before this.

"He went in there," said Tim. "He couldn't help it, no matter how great his hurry."

"I am half disposed to believe you; at any rate let us follow it some ways."

Terror was running over the ground, as though he had made a discovery, and he finally whisked forward out of sight.

"That looks as if he were upon his trail."

"Yis, or somebody ilse's; maybe some of the rid gintlemen has took his marnin' walk in this direction."

They followed the path with caution, and were surprised the

further they advanced. It wound around and among the rocks, which came so close together as to forbid the passage of a man, and the sides never withdrawing more than a dozen feet.

"It looks as though it had been made on purpose," said Tim, gazing around him in admiration.

Finally, it was broken up among the hills, after winding through every point of the compass for fully an eighth of a mile. It gradually rose from its commencement—occasionally interrupted by sharp ascents—until its termination, when they found they had reached no mean elevation.

Still the rocks rose on every hand, and shut out their view of the surrounding country, but showed them a specimen of the wild scenery produced in California. The interior of the hills was cut up by chasms, gorges and ravines, and they heard, but did not see, the rush of a small stream of water.

They stood in silence a few moments and then Howard said:

"If he is lost in here there is no need of us looking for him."

"And why not?"

"We might search till we died of old age, and never find the least trace of him."

"And might discover the poor youngster's body the first half-hour we spint in looking."

This last remark caused Howard to start off at once, fully resolved not to pause again in the search until compelled to do so.

Terror was constantly commanded to hunt for the trail of the boy, and the dog appeared to understand what was expected of him, for he was running constantly hither and thither, but never gave sign that he had found anything positive.

This fact led Howard to doubt whether Elwood had preceded them in this place. If he had really been here, he must have passed directly over the spot upon which they were standing, and it seemed hardly possible that the dog could miss the scent. So strong was he impressed with this that he proposed to Tim O'Rooney to turn back and resume their search outside the hills; but he was so sure that Elwood Brandon could never have passed unentered such an inviting opening that he would not consent to withdraw until they examined further.

Looking around they saw several paths by which they could enter the wild, desolate-looking scene before them. Of course, it was all a matter of chance whether they took the one which had been followed by their lost friend. Tim affirmed that the one that looked the most dangerous and uninviting was surely the right one; but Howard was hardly prepared to admit this. Selecting the most accessible, they carefully followed it for over an hour. In and out among the rocks, sometimes over their tops, then between or around them, down through ravines, and then along their edges, up the stony, earthy sides of the gorges, until at length they halted as they believed in the very heart of this wild looking place.

"Here we are!" said Howard. "I don't see how we can advance much further without going out to the other side."

"It's the qua'rest sight I iver looked upon," said Tim, turning round and round, meaning the wild scenery.

Edward S. Ellis

"But there is nothing learned of Elwood."

"Niver a sign do I saa of the youngster," rejoined Tim. "I graive to think we cannot be near him."

"We have gone on the wrong track."

"I'm a feared so."

"Too bad, too bad," wailed Howard, "what is to come of the poor fellow?"

"But we can't till," hastily added Tim, "do yees put your fingers in your mouth and give that jolly little whistle."

Howard Lawrence was in the very act of doing so when his arm was suddenly arrested by his companion, who, with an exclamation of surprise pointed to a ledge of rocks above them.

# CHAPTER XL

## THE END OF THE SEARCH

About a hundred and fifty feet above them, almost perpendicularly upward, stood an antelope, its small neck outstretched, and its dark, beautiful eyes fixed upon them with a wondering expression. It was on the very edge of a projecting rock where one step more would bring it over.

"It is jist the jintleman we wants," whispered Tim, fearful that he would alarm the timid animal. "We've ate but once in twenty-four hours, and I've jist learned from me stomach that it would have no objection to breaking the same fast; so do yez jist kape still till I pops him over."

"Can you hit him?" asked Howard, scarcely less excited than his companion.

"Be aisy now till ye see the scientific manner I takes to doot."

"Well, be quick, for he is likely to vanish any moment."

Tim O'Rooney carefully sighted his rifle, took a quick, steady aim, and pulled the trigger. Howard, who was keenly watching the antelope, saw it spring up, and as it came down

Edward S. Ellis

it missed the cliff and fell almost at their very feet with a violence and crash which must have broken half the bones in its body.

"Arrah now, an' wasn't that done nicely?" exclaimed Tim, in great exultation, as he ran up to the animal with his knife.

"Are you going to dress it?"

"Yis; an' do yez gather what sticks an' stuff ye can, an' we'll have him cooked in a jiffy."

Howard set about it, for he understood the wisdom of providing themselves with food in the prosecution of this hunt, which in all probability would employ them for some time to come.

"Now, I will give the signal," said he, when his work was completed. "If he is within hearing he will answer it."

"Yis; do your bist, while I pays my respects to this gintleman, an' do ye do the listenin' while ye are about it, for I'm so taken up with this job that I haven't the time to attend to that aither."

Howard strained his cheeks nearly to bursting, and completely exhausted himself in giving forth those ringing screeches which seem to come natural to all school-boys, and are made by uniting the ends of two fingers, inserting them between the lips, and blowing with all the might.

He listened—listened—listened—and then repeated the signal with a desperate fierceness that left him no strength at all; but all in vain—the echoes died away among the rocks and hills, but no answer came back.

"It's no use," remarked Tim O'Rooney, who despite what he had said was listening as earnestly as his young friend.

"The youngster don't hear us. We've got to make a hunt through this old place, and afore we begins it we'll take something for the stomach's sake."

The fire was kindled in the usual manner, and the dinner was not unskillfully prepared by the Irishman. They ate all they could hold. The dog did the same. Tim lit his pipe, and then declared that he was ready for any duty that might be required of him.

As they rose to their feet they were somewhat alarmed at the appearance of the sky. It was overspread with dark, threatening clouds, from which issued rumbling peals of thunder and arrowy lines of lightning. They became darker and more tumultuous each moment, until semi-darkness shrouded them.

"We are going to have a storm," remarked Howard.

"Yis; and a good-sized one, too."

"We shall have to find shelter for ourselves. If much rain falls, this gorge looks to me as if it will be filled with water."

"Worrah, now, but yez are a smart child!" exclaimed Tim O'Rooney, looking admiringly at the boy. "Scarcely mesilf would have thought of the same, and what a credit, therefore, that it should have come into your own."

"I see nothing so wonderful about that. Almost any one would see the danger we are in if we remain here when there is much rain falling. It is just the place for a stream of water."

"So it is—so it is; and yez can saa that there has wather been running over the stones upon which we are standing."

The storm which was so near at hand admonished them to lose no time in seeking shelter. This was a matter of small difficulty, as in such a wild, rugged place there were any number of retreats. They clambered up the path and over the rocks until they reached a point higher yet than where the antelope had stood when pierced by the bullet that had tumbled him over the cliff. They had brought a goodly portion of his meat with them, for there was no telling when they would dare fire a gun again.

A gaping, overhanging ledge, which fortunately was turned from the direction of the storm, was selected as their house, and here they and the dog nestled and waited for the storm to burst. A few large drops that cracked smartly upon the rocks and stones, was the herald of the coming deluge; and then, at the same moment, with a terrific flash and report, came the rain in torrents.

They stood and watched the storm as it raged, and when there was a momentary cessation Howard threw his blanket over his head and said:

"I will run out to the edge of that rock and see whether there is any water in the place where we took our dinner."

"Be careful yez don't tumble over," admonished Tim, feeling it his duty to say something.

"Never fear."

Howard stepped hastily to the spot and looked carefully over. A tiny stream was just beginning to run through the path they had occupied, which was increasing each moment, and would speedily reach the proportions of a torrent. But, although he saw this, there was something which interested him still more, and that was a party of five Indians attentively examining the remains of the antelope, and the signs around it, as if they were seeking their explanation. They looked down to the ground, and two of them pointed precisely in the direction which Tim and Howard had taken in leaving the place.

The rain began falling again more copiously than ever, but Howard would not have heeded it had he not been shrouded in the water-proof blanket. Those Indians had found their camp-fire and were at that moment discussing the best method of capturing him and Tim; but the rain came down so furiously that they finally darted away to seek shelter, and Howard thereupon hurried back to his friend and told him all that he had seen.

"That settles the matter," he added. "Elwood is in their hands, and if we aint careful we shall be with him, for they are searching for us."

"But they can't find us—that they can't."

"Why not?"

"This rain will wipe out our tracks as aisy as if yees had taken a cloth and done it yourself."

"That is true."

Howard was greatly relieved when he reflected that this was true, and that he and Tim were in no danger of capture from being pursued.

The storm lasted several hours, and when it was finished

Edward S. Ellis

they came cautiously forth and made their way stealthily back to where they had left the canoe. They had deliberated long and earnestly regarding Elwood Brandon, and neither of them had any doubt but what he was in the hands of Indians. They had little fear of his being put to death, but believed he would be held a prisoner until either rescued by Shasta, or a party could be sent from the nearest post to ransom him. They had concluded to make all haste homeward and adopt this method of rescue.

And now, as they had given him up for a while, it is high time we took him in hand.

# CHAPTER XLI

## A BOY LOST

When Elwood Brandon separated from Howard Lawrence on the afternoon of their ramble in the woods, it was with the firm intention of making all haste around the range of hills, and there to unite with him in their hunt for Tim.

But, like too many boys, he suffered himself to be led from the sure path by the allurements of the false one. His example furnished a striking moral lesson, which he will doubtless remember to the day of his death.

When we are following the course which conscience tells us is the true one, although it may be rough and stony, and at times most difficult to keep, yet the knowledge of what awaits us at the end should be proof against temptations to turn aside. Woe to him who chides the voice of conscience and listens to that of the charmer!

Elwood had gone some distance, and was walking very rapidly, when he came abruptly upon the opening in the rocks which has been mentioned in another place.

"Ah! here is a shorter cut across," was his reflection as he saw it, and not stopping to think further, he turned and

Edward S. Ellis

walked rapidly through it. "I will beat Howard," and he smiled at the thought. "What will he think when he gets around to see me waiting for him? I know he will run so as to be there first."

Thus hopeful, Elwood hurried forward, thinking only of the surprise he would give his cousin when they met again. As he found the path taking a most sinuous course, a dim idea came through his head that perhaps after all he had not gained so much by "cutting across." He would have turned back as it was but for the rapidly increasing darkness and the belief that he must speedily emerge from the eastern side of the hills.

While walking through a narrow part of the path, he was alarmed by the rattling of some dirt, stones and debris over his head, and before he could retreat or advance he was stricken on the head by several pieces with such violence that he staggered and fell to the ground.

He was not senseless, but somewhat stunned, and placed his hand on his head to see whether it was cut. Finding no blood, he arose to his feet and replied to the whistle of Howard, which had been ringing in his ears for the last ten minutes.

Immediately after, he was taken with a sickness at the stomach, the result, doubtless, of the mental shock received. Such was his faintness and nausea that he lay down upon the ground for relief. When a boy feels so sick—as shown also by older persons in seasickness—he generally becomes perfectly indifferent to everything else in the world. Elwood concluded that Howard might whistle as long as he chose, and he would reply when he felt able. As for the gathering darkness, wild animals and savages, what did he care for them? They could exist and get along without his taking any trouble to think about them.

And so he lay still until his sickness diminished and was gradually succeeded by drowsiness, which was not long in merging into slumber.

Whoever yet remembered the moment he went to sleep? Whoever lay still to gain a few moments of slumber without obtaining far more than he expected, and regretting it when his intellect became sharp and clear?

It was near midnight when Elwood awoke, and all was blank darkness. He called to Howard and Tim, and not until he had felt around with his hands, did he remember his situation. Then it all came to him.

"This is a pretty piece of business," he thought, as he arose to his feet. "Poor Howard is half-frightened to death, and I suppose is still hunting for me. But I don't hear him."

He listened, but all was still.

"It may be that he has grown tired, but will hear me if I call to him."

Whereupon he whistled again and again, and shouted and listened and then repeated his signals, but there was no response. But for the intervening hills his cry would have reached the two watchers by the river shore, but with twice the penetrating power he still would have failed to reach them.

"Well, the best thing I can do is to wait here until morning, and then I can make my way back again."

His sickness was gone, but he felt somewhat chilled from lying upon the ground with no extra covering, although the night was quite moderate, if not really warm. The contact with the ground had made a portion of his body cold, and the sluggish circulation prompted him to exercise.

"I hardly know whether to stay here or to go back to the woods and take refuge in a tree. Some animals may find me here, while I shall be safe if I am only twenty feet above ground."

The vivid recollection of the wolverines gave him this fear and finally induced him to leave the place and seek shelter.

But at the moment of starting he was confronted by an alarming difficulty. He found it impossible to decide upon the proper course to follow, and could not tell with certainty which way led in or out. This resulted from his having turned around several times in his effort to restore warmth and circulation on awaking from his sleep. Had he not done this the position in which he lay during slumber would have told him the truth.

"How strange!" he reflected, vainly seeking to recover from his bewilderment. "If I only had a little light I think I could tell, but this is rather delicate business when I don't know whether I may go over the rocks or not."

He leaned against the wall of the path and thought. At last he believed he knew which way to turn, and facing backward he began to pick his way out. This, we may say, was the right course, and had he only persevered in it would have brought him out of the hills into the woods, restored him to Tim and Howard a few hours later and saved him one of the most momentous experiences of his life.

He had retreated but a few rods when he became sure he had made a mistake and was going wrong. It seemed from his contact with the rocks and the curious windings it made, that he had never passed over the ground, but was advancing further into the hills.

"This will not do," he said aloud, as he paused. "I am astray and must change about."

He did so at once, and believing, of a surety, that he was now upon the right path he walked much faster than was prudent. The truth was, the associations of the plate were such as to make him in a hurry to get away from it. He knew he would feel relieved when he could get once more into the open air of the woods. A strange fear that the overhanging rock would fall or imprison him caused him to hasten still more. After walking some time further he slackened his steps.

"I must be pretty near the opening, judging by the distance I have come; and if such be the case—"

Further words were checked, for at that instant Elwood stepped off the path and went down—down!

## CHAPTER XLII

## A DREARY NIGHT

Elwood fell about twenty feet, striking the solid earth, without losing his own perpendicular position. He was considerably pained, but not seriously hurt. His rifle had fallen from his hand, and was not found again until daybreak, as not knowing where he stood, whether upon the edge of some precipice or ravine, he scarcely dared move a limb.

Ah! if the night was so weary to the watchers by the river shore, it was much more so to him for whom they thus lay awake. Utter midnight blackness all around, the profound and impressive stillness made more profound and impressive by the trickling of some current near, the occasional glimpse of some tiny star twinkling among the dark, straggling clouds overhead; such was Elwood Brandon's situation and surroundings.

His only resource was thought, and the direction which this took for a time was anything but a relief. He saw that he himself was to blame for the disaster of the day. It was he who proposed this ramble, and he who insisted so strenuously upon separating from Howard in the journey around the hills. And then his present situation resulted wholly from his own foolishness—to call it no milder term—

in entering an unknown path with the simple hope of reaching a designated point a few minutes in advance of his friend, whom he knew well enough had carried out to the letter their agreement, and was waiting his coming.

Had Howard found Tim O'Rooney? That was the next question. Or was he still lingering on the other side of the hills, waiting for the morning to renew his hunt for himself before he sought out his companion? The latter seemed the most probable supposition to Elwood, and the odd whim took him that his cousin was close at hand and listening for the familiar signal. So he placed his fingers to his mouth and repeated the whistle which they had used so many times between them.

He did this again and again, but there was no response, and he finally concluded that it was rather a monotonous manner of passing the time and ceased, and again gave himself up to thought.

If he ever lived to see his friends at home what an experience would be his to tell! The burning steamer, the hours spent in drifting ashore, the wanderings through the wilds of California, this adventure among the hills—surely they were enough to last a life-time.

Now and then a cold draft of wind swept by him, as though the temperature of the air was changing. It was in fact the premonition of the gathering storm to which we have referred in another place.

Elwood had been in his constrained position a couple of hours when he was subjected to a terrible fright. Suddenly some dirt and stones commenced moving near him and he felt it strike his feet. He was fearful that a landslide was about to take place, but did not dare attempt to get out of the way. He could only shrink closer against the rocks, pray to Heaven for protection, and await the issue.

The pebbles rattled around him for a long time, and when they had nearly ceased he learned that the whole tumult was caused by some wild animal. This dissipated all fear of being engulfed by a landslide, but scarcely relieved him. It was simply a change of species in the danger.

He could hear the footsteps of the animal as it walked back and forth. They sounded above his head, but he could not judge with certainty. Several times it gave a low growl, from which he was sure that it was dangerous, and if it knew of his presence and could reach him would speedily end his reckless conduct forever.

The animal was still for a while and the boy was indulging in the belief that it had gone, when he heard its footsteps so near that his hair fairly rose with terror. He stooped down and felt around in the darkness for his gun, but it was not within reach. He caught a huge stone and held it in reserve for defense.

Straining his eyes through the darkness, he fancied he could see a dark object above him; but it was only fancy, for to his excited imagination the most extraordinary phantoms were flitting before him—floating in the air, around and above him, like the wonderful visions that visit us in delirium—until he closed his eyes to shut out the tormenting figures.

Perhaps, after all, the presence of the wild animal was the means of saving him, for it kept his mind down to the hard, practical fact that imminent danger was close at hand, and all his thoughts were needed to meet it. He stood a long time grasping the stone and expecting the assault; but the tumult finally ceased and all became still.

When Elwood looked up again he saw that it was growing light, and day was indeed breaking.

# CHAPTER XLIII

## WANDERINGS

The light increased each moment, and Elwood Brandon soon saw the position in which he was placed. He had walked along the path and fallen abruptly off, alighting on a projection that ran along the edge of the ravine, and was of sufficient width to only comfortably hold him. Had he gone a yard forward he would have fallen over to another ledge, although this was not more than a dozen feet below. Indeed, his rifle had done this, and now lay on this broad band of earth and gravel, which here sloped so gradually down to the bottom of the ravine that it could be descended without difficulty.

His first proceeding, after thanking Heaven for the protection of the night, was to let himself down to where his rifle lay. An examination proved it uninjured, and with its possession came a feeling of confidence and safety such as he had not felt for a moment during the hours of darkness.

"Now, if that wild creature, whatever it was, would like to introduce itself, I am prepared."

And he looked around as if he expected its appearance; but it had left some time before. At first he was at a loss to understand what it had chosen as its parade ground, but, concluded it must have been the very path from which he had fallen, and where, had he remained, he could not have avoided falling into its power.

Elwood could not see the possibility of extricating himself by the same way in which he had entered. In some places it was necessary to climb a score or two feet up the perpendicular side of the ravine; and as there was no means at hand for doing this, he thought it best to press on down among the hills in the hope of discovering a new way of egress, or an easier access to the paths behind him.

He wandered rather aimlessly forward, his path being over loose, rattling stones, constantly descending, until he reached the hard-packed earth, and judged himself to be in about the lowermost part of the valley. On every hand rose the ridges, rocks and peaks of the hills, until, as he looked up at the cloudy sky so far above him, he seemed but the merest pigmy.

As he turned his head he caught sight of something a few rods ahead that puzzled him. For some time he could not make out its meaning, but finally he saw that it was a smouldering camp-fire, while around it were stretched five Indians—although at the moment he could not be positive as to their number—their blankets over them and they seemingly sound asleep.

He concluded that the best thing he could do was to leave that immediate neighborhood as speedily as possible. He looked hurriedly around for the best line of retreat. It was difficult to decide, and he was still debating with himself when, as he glanced at the terrifying forms, he fancied, or really saw, one of them move. Without further reflection he darted a rod or two backward and shrunk in behind a breach

Edward S. Ellis

in the rocks.

This was no hiding-place in case the Indians came along this path. He could not conceal his body, as it was merely a niche such as would have been made had this portion of the rocky wall been set back about a foot from the rest. If the savages left the ravine by another direction there was no cause for fear, but if they came this way he had good reason to tremble.

He had scarcely ensconced himself in this place of refuge when from the woods and rocks above him came the clear, echoing whistle of Howard Lawrence. It startled him as if it were the whoop of this Indians so close at hand. Of course he dare not reply to it, for it could only precipitate his capture.

But he trembled more for the safety of his friends than himself. They were advancing hurriedly in their search, without one suspicion of the enemies so near them. Had he dared, to make a noise it would have have been one of warning for Tim and Howard to hasten away ere it was too late; but even that small comfort was denied him.

He peered cautiously out and saw that the Indians were awake, but curiously enough appeared to pay no heed to the whistling, which to the boy were uttered twenty times as often and as loud as there was any need. One of the savages was stirring the fire with a stick, while the others were looking stupidly on.

Drawing back his head, Elwood looked up among the rocks in the direction of the signals for some sign of his friends. He was startled into a suppressed exclamation by the sight of Tim O'Rooney's hat and face passing along the path above him; but before he could catch his eye it was gone and he saw it no more.

The whistling sound now gradually retreated until it sounded quite far away, and Elwood began to feel more at ease, although not entirely so. He wondered greatly that the suspicions of the Indians were not excited, and that they did not hasten away at once to destroy his friends.

The report of Tim O'Rooney's gun that slew the antelope sounded fearfully near, and sent a shiver of terror through the youngster crouching in his hiding-place. At the same time, as he looked stealthily out, he saw that it had attracted the attention of the Indians. All five were standing on their feet, with their loose blankets hung over their shoulders, and gesticulating with their arms. The sound of their voices was plainly heard where he stood, and a thrill of hope ran through him as he imagined that he recognised in one of them a resemblance to that of Shasta, the Pah Utah.

At this point the boy observed the storm gathering overhead—the sullen booming of thunder, the black clouds sweeping tumultuously across the sky, the vivid spears of lightning darting in and out among them. A cool wind whistled through the gorge overhead, and dust and leaves came whirling in the air and settled all around him.

The boy looked above, and saw that when the storm did burst it was sure to spend its full fury upon his head. Not the least particle of shelter covered him, and he had to expect a full drenching; but this he was willing to bear, if it would only tend to keep the attention of the Indians diverted. It seemed to him very probable, as he stood between them and his own friends, that in following up the suspicious report of the rifle they would pass directly by him, in which case he had about one chance out of a thousand of remaining unseen by them.

Elwood did not dare to look out, so fearful was he of being

Edward S. Ellis

seen. He believed that the heads of the savages were turned toward him, in which case the risk was too great. He therefore, unheedful of the large drops that were beginning to patter around him, stood and listened.

Hark! He hears their tread! His heart throbs faster than ever, as he knows they are coming toward him! Closer and closer he shrinks to the rock, as if to bury himself in its flinty surface.

All at once, an Indian, too tall and muscular to be Shasta, steps to view and passes beyond him without turning his head; the second is about the right height, but the one furtive glance stole at him shows that he is a stranger; so as regards the third; the fourth is too short, he passes on in the procession. The fifth and last Elwood at first believed to be Shasta, but a second look showed him his mistake. Had he held any doubts they were removed by the Indian abruptly pausing, turning his face full toward him, and uttering the *"hoogh!"* of surprise, as he saw the boy cowering against the rocks.

## CHAPTER XLIV

## A OLD ACQUAINTANCE

The instant the hindmost Indian uttered his exclamation of surprise, the others paused, and thus, before Elwood Brandon fully realized his danger, he found himself confronted by the whole force. Resistance or flight was not to be thought of, so he merely stood still and tremblingly awaited their will regarding him.

They were plainly surprised at finding a boy pressing against the rooks with an appearance of the greatest terror, and they gazed at him a moment as if uncertain what to do about it. However, they didn't seem to be particularly savage or blood-thirsty, nor frightened, as they kept their guns in their hands and their knives in their belts.

He who stood nearest to Elwood reached out his brawny arm, grasped him firmly and drew him out from his hiding-place. All then scrutinized him as if to make sure whether he was some wild animal or human being. Satisfied on this point, the boy was then shoved forward so as to be between the savages, and as they stepped off he was motioned to do the same. Elwood understood that he was a prisoner, and he philosophically submitted to his fate.

Edward S. Ellis

As yet they had not disturbed his weapons; but he had gone a short distance only when the Indian directly behind him placed his hand upon the muzzle of the gun which was protruding over the youngster's shoulder and began drawing it. The latter disliked very much to part with the rifle, and held it as tightly as possible; but as the savage only drew it the more powerfully, he finally let go and it instantly went from his possession.

Elwood could not forbear looking around at the one who had thus deprived him of his property. As he gazed into his face he was at a loss to understand the expression. The Indian fixed his black eyes upon him, but his lips were closed and not a feature moved or twitched. The boy could not withstand the fierceness of those orbs and was glad to turn his head again.

They walked quite rapidly up the path, making a turn that gave them a very steep ascent. The thunder was booming louder than ever, and the rain by this time was falling furiously. The party hurried forward until they reached the camp which Tim O'Rooney and Howard had so recently deserted. Here Elwood took the liberty of protecting himself by backing against the overhanging rock. This was precisely the position which he occupied when Howard Lawrence gazed over and missed seeing him by such a narrow chance.

When the descent of the rain became so copious as to scatter the savages, two of them ran up beside Elwood and imitated his action in protecting himself from the descending deluge. This was only a partial success, yet much preferable to standing in the open air and receiving the full pelting of the storm.

It will be remembered that Howard Lawrence waited until he saw the Indians hurry away for shelter, when he returned to

Tim O'Rooney and the two effected a safe retreat from the dangerous locality. They saw nothing more of the savages, and their conjecture that Elwood was a prisoner among them was merely a conjecture, although absolutely correct.

The tiny stream running so quietly at the feet of the two aboriginal Americans and Elwood Brandon increased so rapidly that it was evident it would speedily become a torrent that would sweep them off their feet, and that the only safety was to effect as speedy an escape as possible. Taking him between them, they started directly up the path in the direction of their companions. The falling rain and splashing water almost blinded Elwood, but he pressed bravely forward until conscious that they were beneath some kind of covering, and looking around, saw that they stood in a sort of cave, and where they had rejoined the three Indians who had fled some time before.

The shelter proved a secure one, although it was reached rather late to be of much benefit to Elwood, who was thoroughly wetted to the skin. He was, however, rather pleased at the lenient disposition shown by his captors. They had not offered him the least violence, rudeness or insult, and appeared to maintain a very indifferent watch over him. He did not believe they intended him any bodily harm, although he trembled at the consequences when they joined another party or should reach their own homes. They probably intended to hold him a prisoner so long as he was no particular trouble to them; but their leniency was more the result of indifference than of genuine kindness—and indifference that would as soon witness death as life, and that would not stretch out the hand to avert the impending doom.

The storm raged with unabated fury for several hours, and the tiny stream, whose murmur could scarcely be heard as it coursed its way through the hills, was now swelled to the dimensions of a torrent, and roared through its course with a clamor almost deafening. A vast amount of water had fallen within the few hours, and it would have been very perilous had any of the party remained where the fire that cooked the antelope was kindled. A yellow stream some six feet in depth rushed furiously through the narrow passage, like some river when compressed into its narrow canyon.

The Indians stood as motionless as the rocks themselves until the storm was over. Each had his blanket slung over his shoulder, extending down to his knees, and effectually protecting their bodies from the rain which had so thoroughly soaked poor Elwood. None of them sported the defiant scalp-locks so common among the more northern Indians; but their long, black, stiff hair, resembling precisely that of a horse's mane, dangled around their shoulders, neck and ears and over their breasts. Mixed in among the hair on the crown were a number of painted feathers, which, having had a touch of rain, drooped down like those of an humbled chanticleer that has been rescued from the river by some kind hand. Their faces being daubed over with green, yellow and red, mixed and mingled with a sublime disregard of proportion, gave their features a peculiarly unnatural appearance, such as we see when we survey our particular friends through differently and highly colored pieces of glass. They were fine specimens of the "noble red man" that are occasionally met with now-a-days; but they are of that species of sights of which it may be said "distance lends enchantment to the view." However, they were happy, for as yet they had not come in contact with civilization, and had had no taste for the white man's "fire-water," that scourge of the aboriginal race, and which seems destined finally to sweep them from the continent.

Elwood occupied himself in looking from one of these Indians to the other, and speculating regarding their thoughts and opinions about himself, of whose presence they seemed so unconscious. Indeed, they scarcely looked at him except when he sneezed, and then their heads shot round as suddenly as if they were moved by machinery and the spasm had let on the steam.

Finally, when the falling of the rain ceased, two of the Indians went out to look for the remainder of their prisoner's party, which they knew, if not already there, had been so recently among the hills. The vast rush of water, of course, had obliterated all signs where they had made any, and they could only hope to find them by discovering the trail made since the storm, or by the sight of themselves.

Not a word did the savages exchange with each other. They appeared to understand what each thought, and what duty was required of them, which duty for the present resembled that of watching and waiting.

As the day wore away the boy began to feel chilly and hungry. His wet clothes were anything but comfortable, and his hollow stomach was a poor protection against the sinking feeling. As his captors showed no disposition to leave the place, or even to change their statue-like positions, he began to grow anxious. He feared an attack of sickness if his wants were not supplied; and after debating with himself a few moments, he walked up to the tallest Indian and motioned that he needed something to eat.

The reply was startling and decisive. The dusky rascal surveyed him sharply a moment, and then drew his knife and raised it in a menacing manner over his head. And thereupon Elwood retreated to his position, and concluded he wasn't quite as hungry as he first imagined.

It is hard to tell what this singular captivity of Elwood

Edward S. Ellis

Brandon's would have eventuated in had not an unexpected diversion occurred in his favor. Just as it was getting dark, the two Indiana who had gone out at the close of the storm returned. They had a companion with them, and we leave our readers to imagine what the boy's feelings were when he recognized in the third his old friend Shasta, the Pah Utah.

# CHAPTER XLV

## A FRIEND IN NEED

When the Pah Utah entered the cave he did not appear to notice Elwood Brandon. The latter attributed this to the semi-darkness in which he stood, and was about to go forward and claim his friendship when something restrained him, and he concluded to wait until the Indian first recognized him.

Shasta exchanged a few words with his friends, and immediately several of them went out in the darkness. When they returned, which was very speedily, they each bore a goodly bundle of sticks and kindlings. In what part of the wide creation they obtained them, directly after such a deluge of rain, it is impossible to tell, but American Indians have a peculiar faculty of doing such odd things.

A few minutes later a blaze sprung out from the center of the bundle placed in the middle of the cave, and when Elwood looked downward toward it, he saw that Shasta was kneeling before the pile engaged in igniting it. As the flame flared out and illuminated the cave, the Pah Utah looked up and met the eyes of Elwood. For an instant, his black eyes were fixed upon him, and then he placed his finger to his lips and looked down again. The boy understood it all. *He didn't know anything of the Pah Utah.*

The fire burned vigorously and soon diffused a genial warmth throughout the cave. It was most grateful indeed to Elwood, who approached and subjected himself to a toasting process. The savages offered no objection, and he soon managed to secure a pleasant warmth, and partially to dry his damp clothes.

He could not prevent himself from continually glancing at Shasta, but he never once caught his eye, and understanding the Indian's wishes, he compensated for this impertinence by staring twice as long at the other hideous visages.

After all the great want of Elwood was food. He had fasted for thirty hours, and was faint and feeble. A month before such severe abstinence would have left him unable to stand; but the severe deprivation and hardship of the last week, united with its firm, buoyant constitution, and his freedom from the degrading use of tobacco, had developed a strength and endurance remarkable in one so young. He felt that he could wait until the next day without a mouthful, and still be able to travel; but the fainting, craving, hollow feeling rendered him uncomfortable and caused more than one longing look around the cavern and in the faces of his dusky-hued friends; but if the Indians understood his suffering they certainly did not care enough about them to give them heed.

His hope was in the Pah Utah, but his situation was such as to deprive him of the expression of this hope. Shasta had given him to understand in an unmistakable manner that for the present they were to remain strangers; and no matter what his distress might be, he dare not disregard this command.

Yet Elwood Brandon believed, if the Indian understood his

case, he would find some means to relieve him, slight though it was. Finally he decided upon his course of action.

Walking up to the tall Indian, who had received his previous request in such a threatening manner, and halting when at a safe distance, he motioned to him for something to place in his mouth. The unfeeling fellow scrutinized the boy a moment, and then coolly turned his back upon him, and acted as though the supplication had not been made.

He was equally unsuccessful with the others, and the refusal of Shasta was made in a most emphatic manner. Glaring at the boy like an enraged tiger, he brandished his knife and sprung toward him with such a curdling yell that the youngster sprung trembling back to the furtherest verge of the cavern, and the eyes of the other Indians were all turned toward the expected tragedy. But Elwood wasn't frightened—not a bit; he understood what it all meant.

The performance was followed by a conversation between Shasta and the tall Indian, who doubtless belonged to the Pah Utah nation or some tribe friendly with them. It's precise import Elwood found impossible to determine, but he could not avoid a feeling of uneasiness when he saw by unmistakable signs that it referred to himself.

It looked very much as though Shasta was urging immediate disposal of the prisoner, and his friend was strenuously maintaining a different action. The Pah Utah showed great excitement, very often turning and gesticulating toward Elwood, and once or twice he look a step or two in that direction, as if he had resolved on a certain and speedy death for him.

Finally, he appeared to yield the point, and turned his back upon his disputant and walked to the fire. As he did so his face was revealed alone to Elwood Brandon, and looking toward him, the boy again saw him place his finger to his lips and give that warning expression, which said as plainly as words, "Don't be frightened; all things are working right!"

This was certainly gratifying, but our young friend was already satisfied upon this point, and would have much preferred a more substantial mark of friendship in the shape of something to supply the craving within. But on the very eve of despair he was delighted to see a couple of Indians— whose absence he had noted for the last half-hour—return heavily laden with fish. These were immediately taken in charge, by Shasta, and the savor of them as they were cooking drove the famishing boy almost frantic.

While he sat with longing eyes, watching the motions of the cook, one of the fat roasted fellows suddenly shot from his hand and fell into the lap of the boy. The Pah Utah did not raise his head, and the act looked as if it were a voluntary one upon the part of the fish to escape the hands of its tormentors—so dexterously was the whole thing done.

Elwood did not stop to thank his considerate friend, but devoured the food precisely in the fashion that a boy attacks a pile of gingerbread which he has been expecting and longing for during a half-day. When he had finished the fish, another in just as prime condition dropped into his lap, apparently from the top of the cave above.

This satisfied his hunger, and he arose to his feet, casting his eyes toward Shasta, and testifying by his looks the gratitude which he dare not express audibly. He remained in the rear of the cavern, patiently waiting the pleasure of the Pah Utah regarding himself.

The Indians completed their meal, and then exchanged a few

words, when they prepared to leave. Elwood watched them with interest, and when the tall fellow motioned for him to come forward, he did so with alacrity, and took him place in the rear of the line which was formed. Glancing back as they were about to start, he saw by the light of the fire that the one immediately behind him was Shasta.

The night was utterly dark—above, below and all around. The hand of the Pah Utah was placed upon his shoulder, as if to guide him aright, and the march began.

Of course it was impossible for Elwood to tell where he was going, but he followed blindly the direction of him behind for a hundred yards, when he knew by the brushing of his hands against the sides that they were passing through a narrow passage. All at once he felt himself seized by an iron grip from behind, lifted from his feet and tossed into the air. He did not fall back in the path they were traversing, but lit lightly upon a ledge, where he concluded to remain until he heard further from the gentleman who had elevated him to that position.

# CHAPTER XLVI

## WHAT SHASTA DID

The night was still, and the regular tramp of the Indians sounded like the march of a file of soldiers, as they passed over the grass-covered earth. Elwood listened, hardly daring to breathe, as the tread grew fainter, fainter, fainter still, then died out; then was revived by a sigh of the night air, and all was still.

The boy raised his eyes and looked upward. Through the dark clouds drifting tumultuously across the sky he detected the glimmer of a star or two, and in that moment of deep solemnity a passage of the Holy Bible came to him.

"They wandered in the wilderness in a solitary way; they found no city to dwell in."

"Hungry and thirsty, their souls fainted in them."

"When they cried unto the Lord in their trouble, and he delivered them out of their distress."

It came from his heart, and he repeated it over again.

How beautiful! How appropriate to the situation! The tears

welled to his eyes, and his heart overflowed at the repeated remembrance of the all-merciful Father, whose eye alone saw him and whose ear alone heard the thankfulness that would find expression.

He fell into a sweet reverie, from which he was awakened by a slight noise below. He leaned his head over the ledge and listened. All at once he heard a soft rush, and the next moment an Indian was holding on to the edge of the tabular-like projection with one hand, while his other was outstretched and placed upon his body.

"Is that you, Shasta?"

"Oogh! Sh-e-asta!"

"All right! I am waiting for you."

The hand closed upon his right arm; he was lifted bodily as if he were an infant, and held in mid-air; and the next instant the Pah Utah dropped lightly to the earth, and the two stood upon their feet. The Indian uttered an exclamation which seemed to be one of inquiry, and the boy made answer in this manner:

"I am ready for anything, Shasta; lead the way."

Instead of allowing him to walk, as Elwood confidently expected, the Pah Utah flung him over his shoulder and then started on a long, loping trot up the path. His extraordinary agility and muscular power made the weight he carried of the same effect as if it were his rifle he was thus transporting.

This rapid progress continued but a few minutes, when he sunk into a walk—one of long strides, such as would have compelled the boy to a moderate run to equal. He could tell that he was going up quite an ascent, but toward what point it was impossible to tell. Occasionally his hand or his foot struck the projecting rocks, and the rush of the wind now and then against his face told when they were passing through the more open space.

Wonderful indeed was the skill of the Pah Utah, that in the dense darkness showed him, just where and just the outlay of strength that would land his young white friend upon the shelf of safety. Equally extraordinary was the woodcraft that brought him back to the precise spot, and enabled him to thread his way through the impenetrable gloom with the surety of the mountain chamois, which bounds over the fastnesses of the Alps at midday.

Elwood was quiescent, for he know whose hand held him upon those brawny shoulders, and he felt that the moccasined foot which touched the earth so lightly was too sure to miss its hold, and the heart throbbing within that dusky bosom pulsated too powerfully with the common humanity of our nature ever to falter or hesitate in its work of love.

This singular means of progress was continued for the better part of an hour, when the Indian paused and placed him gently on his feet. The sky, which had partially cleared, enabled him to see that they had emerged from the ridge of hills whose entrance had been so eventful to him, and they now stood in the open woods.

Elwood Brandon admitted to himself that the work of Shasta was now finished, and he fully expected to be left alone in the forest to seek his way back to his friends; but if *he* thought so the Pah Utah certainly did not.

Even in that moment the boy could not fail to notice that the

Indian's breathing could not be heard. Not the slightest panting nor exhaustion from the tremendous exertion undergone!

Shasta waited but a moment, and then gripping Elwood by the wrist he began threading his way through the forest. As he did so, instead of allowing the youngster to walk by his side, he held his arm backward, so that to all intents and purposes the boy was following behind him, and yet at such an angle that their feet did not interfere with each other.

Not once did either the Pah Utah or his dependent strike a tree. Often did they graze the back, and brush through the limbs and undergrowth, but the uplifted arm of the Indian parted asunder the obstructions, and opened the way, as does the snow plow of the locomotive to the engine that drives it forward and the train coming behind.

Whether the marvelous vision of the Pah Utah penetrated the Egyptian darkness or not, cannot be said. The veteran backwoodsman, as he strides through the midnight forest, seems to *feel* the presence of each tree-trunk as he approaches it, just as the fingers of pianists strike the piano keys with such bewildering certainty, without their once looking at them.

Onward they pressed, Elwood only now and then able to catch a glimpse of his faithful guide, who never vouchsafed a word or exclamation for his benefit. There was no need of it. Both fully understood each other, and the boy did not attempt to divert the attention which was so needed, at the present time, for the work before him.

Finally Shasta seemed to hesitate—not the hesitation of doubt and uncertainty, but as if he had neared if not reached his destination, and had slackened his pace that he might not pass the exact point.

He was not long in finding the proper spot, and Elwood could see that he was stooping down and busy at something. While he was closely scrutinizing him, he suddenly became aware that they stood beside the river, and the Pah Utah was engaged with his canoe. It occupied him but a moment, when he turned around, lifted the boy over and laid him down upon the blanket which was spread over the bottom of the boat, the remainder was folded carefully around his body, and then the Indian stood back, as if to command his young friend to go to sleep without any delay or questioning.

The boy had lain but a short time when he found the blanket so intolerably warm that he threw a portion from him. It was instantly and rather roughly replaced—evidence that Shasta meant that his wishes should be obeyed. At any rate the boy thought so, and dared not repeat the act.

The great warmth of the blanket caused Elwood to break out into a copious perspiration from head to foot, and caused him almost to gasp for breath; but when he seemed only to meditate on relieving himself of the superabundant clothing, the dusky watcher leaned forward to see whether he dared violate his implied commands. It looked very much as though the Pah Utah was acting as a physician to his youthful friend.

# CHAPTER XLVII

## STILL WAITING

Tim O'Rooney and Howard Lawrence, after making their way out of the range of hills to the river-side, where their canoe lay, waited until dark, in accordance with their agreement, before venturing out upon the river. They were quite uneasy, and to prevent their trail revealing them they dropped a few hundred yards down the shore, where they awaited the coming of darkness.

"Worrah! worrah!" said Tim with an immense sigh, "this is a bad day when we came to leave the youngster with the rid gintleman. A fine youngster was the same—bowld and presumin'. It's a qua'ar failin', Masther Howard, that comes to me."

"Yes, I am sad enough, too."

"Ah! but it is not exactly that be the towken of another faaling intirely."

"What is it then?"

"Whin it's yourself that is lost and awandtherin' off by yourself all alone, and nobody with yees, then I thinks it's

Edward S. Ellis

yees that I loves more nor him that stays with me. But now, whin it's Elwood—God bless him!—that's gone, he's dearer to me than all the rest of the world, not exceptin' yourself. But," and Tim scratched his head in great perplexity, "it's the same that puzzles me sorely. Could yees be afther accounting for it?"

"Elwood and I both know that you think a great deal of us, and no doubt it is because your affection is so equally divided."

"That's it. Yees have made it all plain. I likes each of yees more than the other, and both of yees a great deal the most, whither be the towken of takin' yees apart or together, or takin' both of yees separate, and also wid each other."

Tim nodded his head again and again, as if to signify that it was clear to his mind. Perhaps it was; but if so, one may doubt whether it was as clearly expressed.

"There's another thing that troubles me," added the Irishman, with one of those great inhalations of breath which seem to fill the entire being.

"What is that?"

"Me pipe has gone out, and I hasn't the maans convanient to relight it."

"That is a small infliction which you can well afford to bear. I am only anxious for the night, that we may speed on our way home to get assistance for poor Elwood."

"Yis, if it's bist."

And just in that exclamation Tim O'Rooney echoed the

sentiments of his companion. Ever since leaving the range of hills, with the resolve to hurry away in search of help, the question had been constantly rising in his mind: "Is it best to do so?"

He tried to put it out of hearing, with the determination that he had already decided; but, as if it were the pleadings of conscience, it would not be stifled, and it came again and again, until when Tim spoke it seemed almost as loud as his.

"I can't make up my mind about that," said he. "When we left the hills I had not a moment's doubt but that he was in the hands of the Indians, where there was great danger of our getting ourselves; but then we are not sure of it, and suppose we go away and leave him wandering through the woods until he is captured or is obliged to give himself up to keep from starving. I imagine him following along the shore of the river looking for us—"

"There! there! do yez shtop! No more for me; I've plenty," and the Irishman drew his sleeve across his eyes, as if he were wiping an undue accumulation of moisture, while Howard Brandon was scarcely less affected at the touching picture which he had drawn, and which he felt might be realized from his own remissness.

"I am sure I cannot tell which is for the best," he added in great perplexity. "If a prisoner, he may be able to get away."

"Yis, yees are right; some dark night he can give the owld haythen the slip, and make thracks for the river."

"And who knows but he has been able to elude them, and is only waiting until dark to hunt us up?"

"Yez are right agin; I was about to observe the same myself."

There was one view of the case, which if it did occasionally force itself upon the attention of Howard, he resolutely refused to utter a reference to it. It was that Elwood had been killed accidentally, or by the savages. That was too terrible a contingency to take definite shape until there was no escaping it, and as all of us know better we won't refer to it again.

"Then he may be in the power of these wandering Indians that took such an interest in the antelope we left lying down among the rocks."

"Yis; yez are correct sure."

"How is it, Tim, that you agree with every supposition I make, no matter bow different they are from each other?"

"Wal, you saas me mind is a little foggy, be the towken that I hasn't had the pipe atween me lips since yesterday. When I'm deprived of that pleasure I finds meself unable to reason clearly."

"That is the first time I have heard that smoke makes a thing clearer."

"Ah! that's the trouble," added Tim, with a desponding shake of his head. "If this bad state of things continyees fur a few days longer, yees'll have to laad me around wid a string, or else taach Terror to do the same, as yez have saan a poor blind man and his dog do."

"You draw rather a woeful picture of yourself. But I suppose you can hold out for a few hours longer, and when it becomes dark, we can make a fire, light your pipe and get far away from it before any of the Indians could reach the spot."

"I think yez are right, but me intellect is working so faably this afternoon, that I faars to tax it too hard lest it topples over and gits upsit intirely. Yis, yez are right."

"Somehow or other I think Shasta is in this neighborhood—"

"So does meself," interrupted Tim, in his anxiety to give assent.

"If he is, he will not forget the kindness of Elwood."

"Never!"

"And whether we wait here or not he will attend to his safety all the same."

"That he will—you may depend on it."

"Then shall we wait here or hurry down the river for help?"

"Both, or aither as yez plaise."

"But, Tim, we must do one or the other."

"Let us slaap and draam over it."

This struck Howard as a good suggestion, as they both needed slumber sorely, and adjusting themselves in the canoe, with the Newfoundland as ever maintaining guard, they were quickly wrapped in deep slumber.

When they awoke it was broad day, and the whining of the dog told them at once that he had detected something suspicious.

# CHAPTER XLVIII

## THE MEETING

Tim O'Rooney and Howard Lawrence, awaking at the same moment, observed the alarming action of the dog. Raising their heads they looked carefully around but could detect nothing unusual. They were so securely drawn under the overhanging shrubbery and undergrowth that they were pretty certain no one else was aware of their presence; but the gaze of the dog being turned toward the river they judged that something must be nearing them from that direction.

Nor were they mistaken. A slight ripple was heard, and the next moment a canoe glided to view. In the center, controlling its movements, sat Shasta, the Pah Utah, and directly behind was Elwood Brandon.

Howard could scarcely believe his eyes. He stared again and again, while Tim rubbed his organs of vision, winked and blinked, as though vainly seeking to recover from the bewilderment of a sudden awaking from sleep. Finally he muttered to himself:

"Heaven save me! me intellect has toppled over intirely by raison of the want of me pipe."

"Elwood! Elwood!" called Howard, leaning forward and pulling the bushes apart.

But secure as they deemed their concealment, the eagle eyes of the Pah Utah had penetrated it, while they were yet several rods apart, and abruptly turning the prow of his canoe to one side, he brought it to rest directly opposite and within two feet of the other boat.

Elwood heard his name and saw his friends the next instant. Reaching forward, he grasped the hands of his cousin and the tears trickled down their smiling faces, while Tim continued rubbing his eyes.

"Am I draaming? as me uncle said when they towld him his grandfather had died and willed him two pounds and a half, or does I raaly see before me the youngster that the rid gintlemin had burned up? Let me faal the baal of yer hand."

The two closed hands, and the joy of both was unbounded. Shasta, at this point, showed a delicacy of feeling that did his heart credit. Joining the canoes together in the old-fashioned manner, he motioned Elwood to enter that of his friends, while he gave his exclusive attention to that of propelling the two.

Of course, now that the three were reunited, they overran each other with questions, exclamations and the interchange of experiences since they had separated. It did not require much time for the voluble tongue of Elwood to rattle on his brief stay with the Indians and the remarkable manner in which Shasta had secured his escape. Howard had but little to tell, and that was soon given, and they were left to speculate and conjecture on the future.

Tim's joy drowned his craving for his tobacco, and as he

joined in the glowing conversation of the boys he made no reference to it.

"I think for the prisent," he remarked, "we won't take any hunts upon shore, especially if aich of us has to go alone. The red gintlemen, for some raisin at all, or more likely without any raisin, have taken a great anxiety to make our acquaintance. As fur meself, I prefers to live upon fish to having these same fellows faading upon me."

"Yes," replied Elwood, "I have learned something during the last few days. It is all well enough to be reckless and careless about danger when we are at home and there is no danger, but it is another thing when we are in these parts."

"As the Frenchman remarked, 'tiger hunting is very fine so long as we hunt the tiger, but when he takes it into his head to hunt us the mischief is to pay.'"

"If Shasta will have the onspakable kindness to tow us along in this shtyle for a few waaks, I think we will cast anchor at the wharf in San Francisco without any loss to passingers and freight."

"He has seen what ninnies we were," said Elwood, "and no doubt will accompany us some distance further when he certainly ought to let us try it alone again."

"Ah! but he's a smart young gintleman, as the acquaintances of Tim O'Rooney used to say when they made the slightest reference to him. Couldn't we persuade him to go on to San Francisco wid us? I think your father would be plaised to take him in as a partner in their business wid them."

"But *he* would hardly fancy the change," laughed Howard.

"He might now. When we should state the sarvices he has rindered to us, it's meself that doesn't think they'd require him to put in a very large pile of capital."

"I am sure if he should prove as keen and sharp in business matters as he does in the way of the woods, he would make one of the most successful merchants in the country."

"It's a pity that he doesn't understand the illegant use of the tongue, that we might confaar wid him. We could lay the proposition forninst him, and he could gives us the tarms to carry wid us."

However philanthropic this might be as regarded the Pah Utah, our friends deemed it hardly feasible to make the attempt to reach his views through the medium of signs.

As for Shasta, he did not once look backward to observe what his passengers were doing. He was propelling his boat through the water with his usual celerity, his head occasionally turning slightly as he glanced first at one shore and then the other, as though looking for some sign or landmark.

The day that succeeded the storm was beautiful and clear, everything in nature wearing a fresh and rosy look, as if refreshed by the needed shower. The current of the Salinas was as clear and crystal-like as though it had not received the muddy contents of a thousand brooks, rivulets and torrents gorged with the debris and leaves of its own valley.

"I am troubled by one sore anxiety."

"What can that be?"

"It is for Mr. Shasta. He seems quite forgetful this morning."

"In what respect?" asked Elwood, who did not see the drift of the Irishman's remarks.

"He hasn't had his breakfast, and he must be faaling a wee bit hungry, and be the same token, he must be the victim of great distress, that he hasn't indulged in the use of his pipe."

As Tim O'Rooney had made similar remarks on more than one previous occasion, it may be that the Pah Utah gathered an inkling of his meaning, for the words were scarce uttered when the canoes were headed toward shore, and a landing speedily made.

A piscatorial meal was provided after the manner already fully given, and when finished the soothing pipe of Tim O'Rooney was produced and enjoyed to its full extent.

But Shasta showed no disposition to wait, or to indulge in the solace of the weed. Motioning to his friends to enter the boat, he towed them to the center of the river, where he loosed the fastenings, and without a word or sign he headed his canoe up stream and sped away.

"He is going home," said Howard.

"He must imagine that we are owld enough to walk alone," remarked Tim as he took the paddle.

"But why not bid us good-by?" asked Elwood.

"As he has already done so," replied Howard, "he doubtless does not believe in adding a postscript."

# CHAPTER XLIX

## HOMEWARD BOUND

Now that our friends were left entirely alone, it became a question whether they should continue journeying by day or night.

"It seems to me that we are approaching a more civilized part of the country," said Howard. "I think there will be little risk in continuing our journey."

Tim industriously used his paddle, and shortly afterward, Elwood pointed to an open space some distance inland.

"Yonder are people, and they look as if they were gathered around a camp-fire at their dinner."

Tim jerked his head around, gave a puff of his pipe and said:

"Rid gintlemen ag'in, and I'll shy the canoe under the bank, and craap along till we gets beyonst thim."

"No, they are not Indians—they are white men," quickly added Elwood.

Edward S. Ellis

A careful scrutiny by all ended in a confirmation of Elwood's suspicion.

"That is good," said Howard, with a pleased expression, "it shows that we are getting beyond the wild country into a neighborhood where white men abound, and where we can feel some degree of safety."

"I suppose they are miners or hunters who are taking their midday meal in the open air," added Elwood, who was still gazing at them.

"Shall we heave too, pitch over the anchor, and s'lute them?" asked Tim.

"No; go ahead, we have no time to spare."

The cheering signs continued. An hour later they descried several white men seated in canoes and fishing near shore. They exchanged the courtesies of the day with them and passed on, growing more eager as they neared the goal.

It would have been no difficult feat of the imagination for one standing on shore to fancy that the cause was a pocket edition of a Hudson River steamboat, so powerfully did Tim O'Rooney puff at his pipe, the whiffs speeding away over his shoulder in exact time with the dipping of the paddle, as though the two united cause and effect. The fellow was in the best of spirits. Suddenly he paused and commenced sucking desperately at his pipe-stem, but all in vain; no smoke was emitted.

"What is the matter?" asked Elwood.

"Steam is out, and the paddle won't go."

"Let me relieve you."

The boy used it with good effect, while Tim shoved his blunt finger into the pipe-bowl, shut one eye and squinted into it, rattled it on his hand, puffed at it again, turned his pockets wrong side out, then put them to rights, and repeated the operation, just as we open the door a half-dozen times to make sure our friend isn't behind it, then gave one of his great sighs and looked toward Howard.

"I put the last switch of tobaccy I had in the world into that pipe, just arter throwing myself outside of that quince of fish."

"Quience?" laughed the boy, "you mean *quintal*."

"Yis, and what's to come of Tim O'Rooney, if he doesn't git some more right spaddily. His intellect toppled all the mornin', and can't stand another such strain, or it'll be nipped in the bud afore it has reached the topmost round at the bar of fame."

"Why, Tim, you are growing poetical," called Elwood over his shoulder, not a little amused at his bewildering metaphors.

"We shall doubtless come across some friends before long who will be glad to supply you."

"Elwood!" called Tim.

"What is it!" he asked, pausing in his paddling.

"If you saas a rid gintleman do yez jist rist till I takes aim and shoots him."

Edward S. Ellis

"Why so blood-thirsty?"

"Not blood-thirsty, but tobaccy thirsty. The haythen deal in the article, and if we saas one he must yield."

Elwood promised obedience, but they saw nothing of the coveted people whom they had been so anxious to avoid hitherto, but a half-hour later Howard said:

"Heigh-ho! Yonder is just the man you want to see!"

A single person dressed in the garb of a miner was standing on the shore leisurely surveying them as they came along. There could be no doubt that he was supplied with the noxious weed, for he was smoking a pipe with all the cool, deliberate enjoyment of a veteran at the business.

"Shall I head toward shore!" asked Elwood.

"Sartin, sartin. Oh that we had Mr. Shasta here that he might hurry to land wid the ould canoe!"

A few minutes sufficed to place the prow of the boat against the shore, and Tim O'Rooney sprung out. The miner, if such he was, stood with his hands in his pockets, looking sleepily at the stranger.

"How do yez do, William?" reaching out and shaking the hand which was rather reluctantly given him.

"Who you calling William?" demanded the miner gruffly.

"I beg yez pardon, but it was a slip of the tongue, Thomas."

"Who you calling Thomas?"

"Is your family well, my dear sir?"

"Whose family you talking about?"

"Did yez lave the wife and childer well?"

"Whose wife and childer you talking about?"

"Yez got over the cowld yez had the other day?"

"'Pears to me you know a blamed sight more about me than I do, stranger."

"My dear sir, I have the greatest affection for yez. The moment I seen yez a qua'ar faaling come over me, and I filt I must come ashore and shake you by the hand. I faals much better."

"You don't say?"

"That I does. Would yez have the kindness to give me a wee bit of tobaccy?"

The sleepy-looking stranger gazed drowsily at him a moment and then made answer:

"I'm just smoking the last bit I've got. I was going to ax you for some, being you had such a great affection for me."

# CHAPTER L

## RESCUED

The miner having made his reply, turned on his heel, still smoking his pipe, and coolly walked away, while Tim O'Rooney gazed after him in amazement. The boys were amused spectators of the scene, and Elwood now called out.

"Come, Tim, don't wait! We shall meet somebody else before long; and as you have just had a good smoking spell, you can certainly wait a while."

"Yes," added Howard, "no good can come of waiting; so jump in and let's be off."

The Irishman obeyed like a child which hardly understood what was required of it, and taking his seat said never a word.

"Let me alternate with you for a while," said Howard to his cousin, "you have worked quite a while with the paddle."

"I am not tired, but if you are eager to try your skill I won't object."

The boys changed places, and while Howard gave his

exclusive attention to the management of the canoe, Elwood devoid himself to consoling Tim O'Rooney in the most serio-comic manner.

"Bear up a little longer, my good fellow. There's plenty of tobacco in the country, and there must be some that is waiting expressly for you."

"Where bees the same?"

"Of course we are to find that out; and I haven't the least doubt but the way will appear."

"Elwood," sighed Tim, "'spose by towken of the severe suffering that meself is undergoing I should lose me intellect—"

"I don't think there's any danger."

"And why not?" demanded the Irishman, in assumed fierceness.

"For the good reason that you haven't any to lose."

Tim bowed his head in graceful acknowledgment.

"But suppose I does run mad for all that?"

"I can easily dispose of you?"

"Afther what shtyle?"

"A madman is always a dangerous person in the community, and the moment I see any signs of your malady all I have to do is to shoot you through the head."

"Do yez obsarve any signs at presint?"

"You needn't ask the question, for the moment it breaks out the report of the gun and the crash of the bullet will give you a hint of the trouble."

Tim laughed.

"Yez are a bright child, as me mother used to obsarve whin I'd wash me face in her buttermilk and smiled through the windy at her. If ye continues to grow in your intellect yez may come to be a man that I won't be ashamed to addriss and take by the hand when I maats yez in the straats."

"I hope I shall," laughed Elwood, "the prize that you hold out is enough to make any boy work as he never did before. I hope you will not wish to withdraw your offer."

"Niver a faar—niver a faar, as Bridget Mughalligan said, when I asked her if she'd be kind enough to remimber me for a few days."

"Tim," added Elwood, after a moment's silence, "we are out of the woods."

"What do yez maan by that?"

"We can see signs of the presence of white men all around us, and we have nothing further to fear from Indians."

At this point Howard called the attention of his companion to a large canoe which was coming around a curve in the river. It contained nearly a dozen men, and was the largest boat of the kind which they had ever seen, and savored also of a civilized rather than a savage architect.

"They are white men," said Howard.

"Do yez obsarve any pipes sticking out of their mouths?"

"One or two are smoking."

"Then boord them if they won't surrender."

"They have headed toward us," remarked Elwood, "and must wish to say something."

A few moments later the two boats came side by side, and before any one else could speak Tim made his request known for tobacco. This was furnished him, and as he relit his pipe he announced that he had no objection to their proceeding with their business.

There were nine men in the larger boat, and all were armed with pistols, rifles and knives. In truth they resembled a war party more than anything else bound upon some desperate expedition.

The boys noticed as they came along, and while Tim O'Rooney was speaking, that several of the men looked very keenly at them, as though they entertained some strong suspicion. Finally one of the men asked:

"Are you youngsters named Lawrence and Brandon?"

"Yes, sir."

Here the questioner produced a paper from his pocket, and seemed to read his questions from that.

"And is that man Timothy O'Rooney?"

Edward S. Ellis

"Timothy O'Rooney, Esquire, from Tipperary, at your sarvice," called out the Irishman from the stern of the canoe, where he was elegantly reclining, and without removing the pipe from his mouth.

"Were you on the steamer—that was burned off the coast of California?" pursued the interlocutor.

"Yes, sir."

"Then you are just the party we are looking for."

"Where do you come from?"

"We are from San Francisco, sent out by Messrs. Lawrence and Brandon in search of their children, whom they learned a few days ago from Mr. Yard, one of the survivors, were left on the coast, having wandered inland at the time the others were taken off by the Relief."

This was to the point.

"It is fortunate for all parties that we met you," added the man with a smile, "for we receive a very liberal reward to bring you back, no matter whether we met you within a dozen miles of San Francisco, or were obliged to spend the summer hunting for you among the mountains, only to succeed after giving the largest kind of a ransom."

"Prosaad," said Tim O'Rooney, with a magnificent wave of his hand, without rising from his reclining position. "We're glad to maat yez, as me uncle obsarved, whin Micky O'Shaunhanaley's pig walked into his shanty and stood still till he was salted down and stowed away in the barrel, by raisin of which Micky niver found his pig agin."

The next day the party reached the outlet of the Salinas River, Monterey Bay, where they succeeded in securing transit to San Francisco, and the two boys were once more clasped in the loving arms of their anxious parents.

Howard and Elwood remained in San Francisco until autumn, when they came East again and entered college, and having passed through with honor they returned to the Golden City, and are now partners in a flourishing business. Tim O'Rooney is in their service, and they both hold him in great regard. He is as good-natured as when "Adrift in the Wilds" with the boys, and his greatest grief is that he has never been able to meet Mr. Shasta, the most "illigent savage gintleman that iver paddled his own canoe."


THE END

# Choose from Thousands of 1stWorldLibrary Classics By

A. M. Barnard
Ada Leverson
Adolphus William Ward
Aesop
Agatha Christie
Alexander Aaronsohn
Alexander Kielland
Alexandre Dumas
Alfred Gatty
Alfred Ollivant
Alice Duer Miller
Alice Turner Curtis
Alice Dunbar
Allen Chapman
Alleyne Ireland
Ambrose Bierce
Amelia E. Barr
Amory H. Bradford
Andrew Lang
Andrew McFarland Davis
Andy Adams
Angela Brazil
Anna Alice Chapin
Anna Sewell
Annie Besant
Annie Hamilton Donnell
Annie Payson Call
Annie Roe Carr
Annonaymous
Anton Chekhov
Archibald Lee Fletcher
Arnold Bennett
Arthur C. Benson
Arthur Conan Doyle
Arthur M. Winfield
Arthur Ransome
Arthur Schnitzler
Arthur Train
Atticus
B.H. Baden-Powell
B. M. Bower
B. C. Chatterjee
Baroness Emmuska Orczy
Baroness Orczy
Basil King
Bayard Taylor
Ben Macomber
Bertha Muzzy Bower
Bjornstjerne Bjornson

Booth Tarkington
Boyd Cable
Bram Stoker
C. Collodi
C. E. Orr
C. M. Ingleby
Carolyn Wells
Catherine Parr Traill
Charles A. Eastman
Charles Amory Beach
Charles Dickens
Charles Dudley Warner
Charles Farrar Browne
Charles Ives
Charles Kingsley
Charles Klein
Charles Hanson Towne
Charles Lathrop Pack
Charles Romyn Dake
Charles Whibley
Charles Willing Beale
Charlotte M. Braeme
Charlotte M. Yonge
Charlotte Perkins Stetson
Clair W. Hayes
Clarence Day Jr.
Clarence E. Mulford
Clemence Housman
Confucius
Coningsby Dawson
Cornelis DeWitt Wilcox
Cyril Burleigh
D. H. Lawrence
Daniel Defoe
David Garnett
Dinah Craik
Don Carlos Janes
Donald Keyhoe
Dorothy Kilner
Dougan Clark
Douglas Fairbanks
E. Nesbit
E. P. Roe
E. Phillips Oppenheim
E. S. Brooks
Earl Barnes
Edgar Rice Burroughs
Edith Van Dyne
Edith Wharton

Edward Everett Hale
Edward J. O'Biren
Edward S. Ellis
Edwin L. Arnold
Eleanor Atkins
Eleanor Hallowell Abbott
Eliot Gregory
Elizabeth Gaskell
Elizabeth McCracken
Elizabeth Von Arnim
Ellem Key
Emerson Hough
Emilie F. Carlen
Emily Bronte
Emily Dickinson
Enid Bagnold
Enilor Macartney Lane
Erasmus W. Jones
Ernie Howard Pie
Ethel May Dell
Ethel Turner
Ethel Watts Mumford
Eugene Sue
Eugenie Foa
Eugene Wood
Eustace Hale Ball
Evelyn Everett-green
Everard Cotes
F. H. Cheley
F. J. Cross
F. Marion Crawford
Fannie E. Newberry
Federick Austin Ogg
Ferdinand Ossendowski
Fergus Hume
Florence A. Kilpatrick
Fremont B. Deering
Francis Bacon
Francis Darwin
Frances Hodgson Burnett
Frances Parkinson Keyes
Frank Gee Patchin
Frank Harris
Frank Jewett Mather
Frank L. Packard
Frank V. Webster
Frederic Stewart Isham
Frederick Trevor Hill
Frederick Winslow Taylor

| | | |
|---|---|---|
| Friedrich Kerst | Hayden Carruth | James Branch Cabell |
| Friedrich Nietzsche | Helent Hunt Jackson | James DeMille |
| Fyodor Dostoyevsky | Helen Nicolay | James Joyce |
| G.A. Henty | Hendrik Conscience | James Lane Allen |
| G.K. Chesterton | Hendy David Thoreau | James Lane Allen |
| Gabrielle E. Jackson | Henri Barbusse | James Oliver Curwood |
| Garrett P. Serviss | Henrik Ibsen | James Oppenheim |
| Gaston Leroux | Henry Adams | James Otis |
| George A. Warren | Henry Ford | James R. Driscoll |
| George Ade | Henry Frost | Jane Abbott |
| Geroge Bernard Shaw | Henry James | Jane Austen |
| George Cary Eggleston | Henry Jones Ford | Jane L. Stewart |
| George Durston | Henry Seton Merriman | Janet Aldridge |
| George Ebers | Henry W Longfellow | Jens Peter Jacobsen |
| George Eliot | Herbert A. Giles | Jerome K. Jerome |
| George Gissing | Herbert Carter | Jessie Graham Flower |
| George MacDonald | Herbert N. Casson | John Buchan |
| George Meredith | Herman Hesse | John Burroughs |
| George Orwell | Hildegard G. Frey | John Cournos |
| George Sylvester Viereck | Homer | John F. Kennedy |
| George Tucker | Honore De Balzac | John Gay |
| George W. Cable | Horace B. Day | John Glasworthy |
| George Wharton James | Horace Walpole | John Habberton |
| Gertrude Atherton | Horatio Alger Jr. | John Joy Bell |
| Gordon Casserly | Howard Pyle | John Kendrick Bangs |
| Grace E. King | Howard R. Garis | John Milton |
| Grace Gallatin | Hugh Lofting | John Philip Sousa |
| Grace Greenwood | Hugh Walpole | John Taintor Foote |
| Grant Allen | Humphry Ward | Jonas Lauritz Idemil Lie |
| Guillermo A. Sherwell | Ian Maclaren | Jonathan Swift |
| Gulielma Zollinger | Inez Haynes Gillmore | Joseph A. Altsheler |
| Gustav Flaubert | Irving Bacheller | Joseph Carey |
| H. A. Cody | Isabel Cecilia Williams | Joseph Conrad |
| H. B. Irving | Isabel Hornibrook | Joseph E. Badger Jr |
| H.C. Bailey | Israel Abrahams | Joseph Hergesheimer |
| H. G. Wells | Ivan Turgenev | Joseph Jacobs |
| H. H. Munro | J.G.Austin | Jules Vernes |
| H. Irving Hancock | J. Henri Fabre | Julian Hawthrone |
| H. R. Naylor | J. M. Barrie | Julie A Lippmann |
| H. Rider Haggard | J. M. Walsh | Justin Huntly McCarthy |
| H. W. C. Davis | J. Macdonald Oxley | Kakuzo Okakura |
| Haldeman Julius | J. R. Miller | Karle Wilson Baker |
| Hall Caine | J. S. Fletcher | Kate Chopin |
| Hamilton Wright Mabie | J. S. Knowles | Kenneth Grahame |
| Hans Christian Andersen | J. Storer Clouston | Kenneth McGaffey |
| Harold Avery | J. W. Duffield | Kate Langley Bosher |
| Harold McGrath | Jack London | Kate Langley Bosher |
| Harriet Beecher Stowe | Jacob Abbott | Katherine Cecil Thurston |
| Harry Castlemon | James Allen | Katherine Stokes |
| Harry Coghill | James Andrews | L. A. Abbot |
| Harry Houidini | James Baldwin | L. T. Meade |

L. Frank Baum
Latta Griswold
Laura Dent Crane
Laura Lee Hope
Laurence Housman
Lawrence Beasley
Leo Tolstoy
Leonid Andreyev
Lewis Carroll
Lewis Sperry Chafer
Lilian Bell
Lloyd Osbourne
Louis Hughes
Louis Joseph Vance
Louis Tracy
Louisa May Alcott
Lucy Fitch Perkins
Lucy Maud Montgomery
Luther Benson
Lydia Miller Middleton
Lyndon Orr
M. Corvus
M. H. Adams
Margaret E. Sangster
Margret Howth
Margaret Vandercook
Margaret W. Hungerford
Margret Penrose
Maria Edgeworth
Maria Thompson Daviess
Mariano Azuela
Marion Polk Angellotti
Mark Overton
Mark Twain
Mary Austin
Mary Catherine Crowley
Mary Cole
Mary Hastings Bradley
Mary Roberts Rinehart
Mary Rowlandson
M. Wollstonecraft Shelley
Maud Lindsay
Max Beerbohm
Myra Kelly
Nathaniel Hawthrone
Nicolo Machiavelli
O. F. Walton
Oscar Wilde

Owen Johnson
P.G. Wodehouse
Paul and Mabel Thorne
Paul G. Tomlinson
Paul Severing
Percy Brebner
Percy Keese Fitzhugh
Peter B. Kyne
Plato
Quincy Allen
R. Derby Holmes
R. L. Stevenson
R. S. Ball
Rabindranath Tagore
Rahul Alvares
Ralph Bonehill
Ralph Henry Barbour
Ralph Victor
Ralph Waldo Emmerson
Rene Descartes
Ray Cummings
Rex Beach
Rex E. Beach
Richard Harding Davis
Richard Jefferies
Richard Le Gallienne
Robert Barr
Robert Frost
Robert Gordon Anderson
Robert L. Drake
Robert Lansing
Robert Lynd
Robert Michael Ballantyne
Robert W. Chambers
Rosa Nouchette Carey
Rudyard Kipling
Saint Augustine
Samuel B. Allison
Samuel Hopkins Adams
Sarah Bernhardt
Sarah C. Hallowell
Selma Lagerlof
Sherwood Anderson
Sigmund Freud
Standish O'Grady
Stanley Weyman
Stella Benson
Stella M. Francis

Stephen Crane
Stewart Edward White
Stijn Streuvels
Swami Abhedananda
Swami Parmananda
T. S. Ackland
T. S. Arthur
The Princess Der Ling
Thomas A. Janvier
Thomas A Kempis
Thomas Anderton
Thomas Bailey Aldrich
Thomas Bulfinch
Thomas De Quincey
Thomas Dixon
Thomas H. Huxley
Thomas Hardy
Thomas More
Thornton W. Burgess
U. S. Grant
Upton Sinclair
Valentine Williams
Various Authors
Vaughan Kester
Victor Appleton
Victor G. Durham
Victoria Cross
Virginia Woolf
Wadsworth Camp
Walter Camp
Walter Scott
Washington Irving
Wilbur Lawton
Wilkie Collins
Willa Cather
Willard F. Baker
William Dean Howells
William le Queux
W. Makepeace Thackeray
William W. Walter
William Shakespeare
Winston Churchill
Yei Theodora Ozaki
Yogi Ramacharaka
Young E. Allison
Zane Grey